A

SAINSBURY COOKBOOK

—

THE COOKING OF
THE USA

PATRICIA LOUSADA

CONTENTS

Published exclusively for J Sainsbury plc
Stamford House Stamford Street
London SE1 9LL
by Martin Books
Simon & Schuster International Group
Fitzwilliam House 32 Trumpington Street
Cambridge CB2 1QY

First published as *American Sampler* 1982
New enlarged edition 1985
Reprinted as *The Cooking of the USA* 1990
Text © Patricia Lousada 1985
Photographs and illustrations © J Sainsbury plc 1985

ISBN 0 85941 466 3

Printed in Great Britain

THE AUTHOR

Lady Lousada was born in New York City. Her Italian mother was a singer and an inspired cook with a wide knowledge of Italian and French cuisine. Patricia was a member of the New York City Ballet and her fellow dancers' love of good food further involved her in cooking. She later lived in Paris for two years, where the experience of attending lectures at the Cordon Bleu school, against a background of Parisian restaurants, deepened her interest still more. She has given lectures and demonstrations on various kinds of cooking.

This book derives from her early nostalgic affection for American specialities. It is her second book for Sainsbury's, the first being *Pasta Italian Style*, now also available in an enlarged edition.

Lady Lousada lives in London with her English husband and has four children.

INTRODUCTION

The cooking of America is as diverse as the mixture of its peoples and the variety of its natural food supplies. Some American dishes date back to the days of the Pilgrim Fathers and others come from the original cuisine of the immigrant groups from Germany, Holland and Scandinavia. In the southern states a distinct cuisine has emerged, influenced by the French and Spanish heritage. A happier part of the slave trade was the arrival, from the West Indies, of exotic spices and flavourings.

When the English and Dutch settlers arrived in the New World they found the American Indians had a varied diet, based on wild game and fish, maize, tomatoes, wild rice, squash and the wild turkey, which they had domesticated. After the failure of their own crop of seeds, brought from the Old World, the settlers were helped by the Indians to grow maize and were saved from starvation. Thanksgiving Day, much the most important American holiday still celebrates their first good harvest.

Learning from the Indians, the settlers discovered the unknown foods of the New World. Pumpkins helped them survive the long New England winters. Wild cranberries and blueberries provided a delicious source of fruit. The settlers were soon tapping the maple trees as the Indians did, for syrup – an early treat still loved by today's New England children is maple syrup and snow 'candy' (when the syrup is poured on snow it hardens and is eaten like candy).

Later, pioneers pressing westwards across the continent took this early New England way of eating with them, and it became staple fare all over the expanding nation. As immigrants came from Northern Europe they brought with them their own customs and cuisines; transformed by indigenous foods these dishes took on a new flavour and continued the varied story of American cooking.

Note on quantities

Ingredients in the recipes are given in both imperial (oz, pints, etc) and metric (g, ml, etc) measures: use either set of quantities, but not a mixture of both, in any one recipe. All spoons are level unless otherwise stated; metric spoon measures, if you follow these instead, are always level. Egg size, where unspecified, is medium (size 3).

Although this book is only a sampler of the wide range of American cookery, I can't resist talking about my favourite foods. The baking of fruit and corn breads, sweet muffins and pies is a special American tradition. When ovens were first manufactured in the United States, they were described as '5-pie' or '10-pie' ovens – or even '20-pie' for the big farming homesteads. Apple pie 'à la mode' is an all-time American favourite and certainly one of mine. The tradition of long, slow oven cooking is also responsible for Boston baked beans and steamed brown bread, a delectable New England treat. Cookies (from the Dutch word *koekjes*) play an important role in American cooking – raiding a cookie-jar full of home-made toll house or peanut butter cookies is a treasured childhood memory of millions of Americans.

To return to New York (where I spent my hungry teens), the variety of exotic dishes that have become familiar American favourites is endless. From Chinese-inspired barbecued spare-ribs, through Jewish hot corned beef sandwiches to Mexican chilli con carne, I enjoyed and still enjoy them all.

I hope that through the recipes in this book you will discover the delights of American cooking and will share their pleasures with your friends.

Vanilla essence

Some of my recipes call for vanilla essence. In America, pure vanilla extract, although expensive, is very widely used in baking. The vanilla flavouring sold in Britain often imparts quite a different flavour from this. A good home-made substitute for vanilla extract is vanilla sugar, easily made by storing one or two vanilla pods in a jar of sugar. Try using this sugar instead of ordinary sugar in recipes that need a vanilla flavour.

SOUPS AND SALADS

CORN CHOWDER

1 lb (450 g) frozen corn kernels

1½ pints (900 ml) water

1 tablespoon (15 ml spoon) dripping or oil

3 oz (75 g) piece of streaky bacon, rind removed, cut into ¼-inch (5 mm) cubes

12 oz (350 g) onions, sliced thinly

3 medium-size potatoes, peeled and cut into ¼-inch (5 mm) cubes

½ pint (300 ml) single cream

½ pint (300 ml) milk

salt and freshly ground black pepper

To garnish:

chopped parsley

A very thick nourishing soup from New England, Corn Chowder makes delicious use of frozen corn. The crisp bacon, potatoes and onions turn it into a meal in itself – ideal for a tasty lunch in winter. Serve it with wholemeal bread and perhaps a salad.

Place half the corn with ½ pint (300 ml) of the water in a liquidiser or processor and whizz together to a smooth purée.

Heat the dripping or oil in a large saucepan and fry the bacon until it is crisp and brown. Remove it with a slotted spoon and put aside. Add the sliced onions to the remaining fat and cook, stirring, until the onions soften. Stir in the corn purée, the remaining corn kernels, the potatoes, salt and pepper and the remaining 1 pint (600 ml) water. Cover and simmer until the potatoes are cooked but still retain their shape, about 15–20 minutes. Add the cream and milk and heat without allowing it to come to the boil.

Before serving, stir in the bacon, taste for seasoning and garnish with the parsley.

NEW ENGLAND FISH CHOWDER

Serves 6 as a main course

1½ lb (675 g) fish heads, backbones and trimmings

6 oz (175 g) salt pork or piece of unsmoked bacon, rind removed, cut into ½-inch (1 cm) cubes

1 tablespoon (15 ml spoon) oil

2 lb (900 g) onions, sliced thinly

2 tablespoons (2 × 15 ml spoon) plain flour

2 lb (900 g) potatoes, sliced thinly

1 teaspoon (5 ml spoon) chopped fresh, or ½ teaspoon (2.5 ml spoon) dried, thyme

1 bay leaf

1½ pints (900 ml) milk

2½ lb (1.25 kg) fresh or frozen cod, haddock or other fish fillets, all one kind or a mixture, cut into 2-inch (5 cm) chunks

salt and freshly ground pepper

To garnish:

8 water biscuits, broken into small pieces

chopped parsley

The name 'chowder' comes from the French la chaudière – a huge copper pot for cooking a communal fish stew. Canadian and northern New England fishermen continued the French tradition of celebrating the safe return of the fleet, with each fisherman contributing something from his catch for the 'chowder'. New England Fish Chowder is a delicious creamy stew with an unusual combination of fish and salt pork, simmered with thinly sliced potatoes and onions. It is a complete meal in itself and perfect for an informal lunch or supper.

Put all the fish trimmings in a large saucepan with 2 pints (1.2 litres) cold water. Bring to the boil and simmer gently for 20 minutes, uncovered. Strain and reserve the stock.

Blanch the pork or bacon in a further 2 pints (1.2 litres) boiling water for 5 minutes. Drain and then place in a large pan with the oil. Fry the meat until it is lightly browned and the fat is melted. Stir in the onions and cook for another 8–10 minutes, stirring frequently. Add the flour and cook together for another 2 minutes. Then add the reserved fish stock, potatoes, thyme, bay leaf and salt and pepper to taste. Cook covered over a gentle heat until the potatoes are just tender (about 15 minutes).

Shortly before you are ready to serve the chowder bring it to the boil and add the milk and the fish fillets. Simmer gently for about 5 minutes, until the fish is just cooked.

Serve in wide soup bowls and sprinkle some biscuit pieces and parsley over each serving.

PUMPKIN SOUP

3 lb (1.3 kg) piece of pumpkin

1 oz (25 g) butter

1 medium-size onion, chopped finely

1 pint (600 ml) chicken stock

½ pint (300 ml) milk

1 tablespoon (15 ml spoon) lemon juice

a pinch of sugar

½ teaspoon (2.5 ml spoon) freshly grated or ground nutmeg or mace

salt and freshly ground black pepper

Oven temperature:
Gas Mark 4/350°F/180°C

Pumpkins are a common sight in the fall in New England. Their lovely orange colour and round shapes look wonderful in the fields – and in the greengrocers. They make very good soup of a beautiful pale orange colour and a delicate flavour, a perfect start to any meal.

Scrape out the seeds and the stringy centre from the piece of pumpkin. Place it skin side up on a baking sheet and bake in the preheated oven for about 45 minutes, until the pumpkin is tender when pierced with a fork. Scrape the pulp from the shell and reserve (you should have about 1½ lb/675 g of pulp). Alternatively, you can cut the peeled flesh of the pumpkin into pieces and cook them in a small amount of water until tender. Add the water with the pumpkin to the other ingredients.

Melt the butter in a large saucepan and sauté the onion in it until tender. Add the chicken stock, milk, pumpkin pulp, lemon juice, sugar and nutmeg or mace. Cover and simmer for 20 minutes. Pass the soup through a mouli or sieve and return to the pan. When ready to serve, reheat and season well with salt and lots of black pepper.

Pumpkin Soup

SPINACH AND BACON SALAD WITH HOT DRESSING

Serves 6

12 oz (350 g) fresh young spinach

2 tablespoons (2 × 15 ml spoon) sunflower oil

8 rashers of streaky bacon, with the rind removed

2 tablespoons (2 × 15 ml spoon) cider vinegar

1 tablespoon (15 ml spoon) fresh herbs (such as chives, chervil or parsley), chopped finely

4 oz (100 g) small mushrooms, sliced thinly

salt and black pepper (optional)

This delicious salad is a favourite in New York City. Crispy bits of bacon with raw spinach is a wonderful combination and the hot dressing magically takes away the sharpness from the spinach. This dish is also good made with watercress or curly endive.

Wash the spinach carefully in cold water. Pull off the stalks and dry the leaves. Cut them into 1-inch (2 cm) strips and place in a salad bowl. If not using at once, cover with a clean, damp cloth and chill in the refrigerator.

Heat the oil in a frying pan and fry the bacon over a medium heat until crisp. Remove with a slotted spoon and chop coarsely. Before serving, add the vinegar and herbs to the fat in the frying pan and gently heat together, stirring. Pour over the spinach and toss together. Add the bacon and mushrooms, and salt and pepper, if liked.

VICHYSSOISE

Serves 6–8

12 oz (350 g) white part of leeks, sliced thinly

12 oz (350 g) potatoes, peeled and sliced thinly

4 oz (100 g) onion, chopped

1¾ pints (1 litre) good home-made chicken stock

½ pint (300 ml) single cream

salt and freshly ground white pepper

To garnish:

3 tablespoons (3 × 15 ml spoon) finely chopped fresh chives

Despite its French name, this cold soup was invented in New York City to commemorate the opening of the roof garden at the old Ritz Carlton hotel in 1910. It is a wonderful soup and excellent hot as well as cold.

Wash and drain the leeks. (Save the green parts for another dish.) Place the leeks, potatoes and onion in a saucepan. Add the stock and simmer, covered, for 35 minutes or until the vegetables are very soft. Sieve or purée in a liquidiser or processor. Stir in the cream and season well with salt and pepper. If you are serving the soup cold, chill and serve in chilled bowls, garnished with lots of chopped chives. If you are serving hot, heat to just below the boiling point before serving, garnished with the chives.

CAESAR SALAD

2 small cos lettuces

4 thick slices of white bread

6–8 tablespoons (6–8 × 15 ml spoon) sunflower or groundnut oil

1 teaspoon (5 ml spoon) garlic, finely chopped

2 eggs

6–8 tablespoons (6–8 × 15 ml spoon) olive oil

3 tablespoons (3 × 15 ml spoon) lemon juice

a dash of Worcestershire sauce

1 oz (25 g) freshly grated parmesan

salt and freshly ground black pepper

Caesar Cardini made this salad famous at his restaurant in Tijuana in the 1920s. He would assemble it before his guests, breaking the eggs over the lettuce and scooping it up theatrically to mix in all the delicious fresh ingredients. It makes a wonderful first course.

Separate the lettuce leaves, wash and dry them and place in a clean cloth in the refrigerator. Cut the crusts off the bread and cut into ½-inch (1 cm) cubes. Heat the oil in a pan; when very hot, add the bread croûtons and fry until golden. Remove the pan from the heat and add the garlic. Stir the croûtons with the garlic in the hot oil and then remove them to kitchen towelling to drain.

   Place the eggs in boiling water and boil for just 1 minute. Remove and set aside. Break the chilled lettuce leaves into pieces and place in a salad bowl. Add the olive oil and a good sprinkling of salt and pepper and toss together. Next break the eggs over the salad, scraping out the partly set white, add the lemon juice and Worcestershire sauce and mix again. Add the cheese and the bread croûtons and give a final toss before serving.

CHEF'S SALAD

1 round lettuce or small
Webb's lettuce

1 small bunch of watercress

4 oz (100 g) sliced cooked
ham, cut into matchsticks

4 oz (100 g) sliced
Emmenthal cheese, cut into
matchsticks

2 eggs, hard-boiled and
quartered

1 oz (25 g) black olives,
stoned and chopped roughly

4–6 anchovy fillets,
chopped

2–3 tomatoes, peeled and
quartered

For the dressing:

2 teaspoons (2 × 5 ml
spoon) Dijon mustard

1 tablespoon (15 ml spoon)
cider vinegar

4 tablespoons (4 × 15 ml
spoon) olive oil, or a
mixture of olive and
sunflower oil

salt and pepper

I lived on salads in my diet-conscious days as a dancer
in New York City and this was one of my favourites.
For an authentic American-style lunch, serve it with
Parker House Rolls (page 49), followed perhaps by a
slice of Pineapple Upside-down Cake (page 63).

Wash and dry the lettuce and watercress and tear
into pieces. Place in a salad bowl with all the
other ingredients. Mix all the dressing
ingredients together. Before serving, pour the
dressing over the salad and toss together.

Chef's Salad; Caesar Salad

TOMATO ASPIC

For the aspic:

2 tablespoons (2 × 15 ml spoon) gelatine

3 fl oz (75 ml) cold water

2 × 14 oz (397 g) can of tomatoes

1 small onion, chopped

1 carrot, chopped

2 sticks of celery, chopped

½ bay leaf

a pinch of dried thyme

2 tablespoons (2 × 15 ml spoon) sugar

1 teaspoon (5 ml spoon) salt

For the filling:

9 oz (250 g) thick-set natural yogurt

½ cucumber, peeled and diced

½ clove of garlic, chopped very finely

4 tablespoons (4 × 15 ml spoon) chopped fresh mint or 2 tablespoons (2 × 15 ml spoon) dried

a pinch of salt

Aspic rings were a great feature at luncheon parties when I was growing up in the States. This tomato aspic is so light and refreshing that it is a perfect first or salad course for today when everyone is health conscious. It can be served on its own or the centre can be filled with cottage cheese and chives, shrimp salad or any number of combinations. I like this cucumber and yogurt one.

Sprinkle the gelatine over the water and set aside. Place all the remaining ingredients for the aspic in a saucepan and simmer very gently, covered, for 30 minutes. Strain the mixture through a sieve into a bowl, pressing out as much juice as possible with the back of a spoon. Measure the liquid and add hot water, if necessary, to make 2 pints (1.2 litres). Add the gelatine and stir to dissolve. (If the tomato juice has cooled down you may have to heat it again gently to dissolve the gelatine, but do not allow it to boil.) Taste for seasoning – it may need more salt or sugar. Pour into a wetted 2-pint (1.2-litre) ring mould and cool before refrigerating.

At least 2 hours before serving, mix all the filling ingredients together. Unmould the aspic by placing the bottom in very hot water for a few seconds and then turning out on to a plate. Fill the centre with the yogurt mixture.

PHIL'S COCKLE CHOWDER

Serves 4–6

¼ green pepper, chopped
finely

1 small stick of celery,
chopped finely

1 medium-size potato,
peeled and diced

1 oz (25 g) butter

3 slices of streaky bacon, cut
into ¼-inch (5 mm) strips

1 small onion, chopped
finely

2 tablespoons (2 × 15 ml
spoon) plain flour

12 oz (350 g) cockles, fresh
or frozen, but not in vinegar
(see Note below)

1 pint (600 ml) milk

salt and freshly ground black
pepper

To garnish:

some parsley, chopped
finely

cream crackers

*Clam chowder is a great speciality up and down the
east coast of New England. Since clams are hard to
come by here, my ingenious American neighbour Phil
Brown devised this very acceptable version.*

Put the pepper, celery and potato in a pan with
just enough water to cover and simmer for about
10 minutes, until the vegetables are tender but
firm. Put the pan to one side. Heat the butter in a
frying pan and sauté the bacon and onion until
they are soft but not brown. Sprinkle in the flour
and cook for a further few minutes.

Place the milk in the top of a double saucepan
(or a bowl over a small pan) over barely
simmering water. Add the vegetables and their
cooking water, the cockles, the bacon and the
onion. Deglaze the frying pan with some of the
milk (scraping the bottom of the pan with a
spoon) and add this as well. When the chowder
is very hot and slightly thickened, but not
boiling, it is ready. Taste for seasoning and serve
garnished with the parsley. The cream crackers
are crumbled up and eaten in the chowder.

Note: the cockles often contain a bit of sand.
You can either ladle the soup out carefully,
avoiding the bottom of the pan where it will
settle, or rinse the cockles well before using. The
disadvantage with the latter is that some of the
flavour is also washed away.

MAIN DISHES AND ACCOMPANIMENTS

PRAWN AND HAM JAMBALAYA

Serves 6

6 fl oz (175 ml) water

2 teaspoons (2 × 5 ml spoon) salt

6 oz (175 g) long grain easy-cook rice

3 medium-size onions

2 cloves of garlic

3 stalks of celery

1 green pepper

2 tablespoons (2 × 15 ml spoon) sunflower oil

1 oz (25 g) butter

14 oz (397 g) can of tomatoes

3 tablespoons (3 × 15 ml spoon) tomato purée

2 tablespoons (2 × 15 ml spoon) finely chopped fresh parsley

½ teaspoon (2.5 ml spoon) ground cloves

½ teaspoon (2.5 ml spoon) dried thyme

½ teaspoon (2.5 ml spoon) cayenne pepper

1 lb (450 g) lean cooked ham, cut into ½-inch (1 cm) cubes

1 lb (450 g) peeled cooked prawns

freshly ground black pepper

Jambalaya was brought by the Spaniards to New Orleans in the late 1700s and the name probably comes from the Spanish word for ham, jamon. The ham, prawns and rice absorb the spicy tomato sauce and make a rich succulent stew. Serve it with a green vegetable or salad.

Bring the water and 1 teaspoon (5 ml spoon) of the salt to the boil in a small saucepan. Add the rice and cover the pan immediately. Simmer over a very low heat for about 10 minutes, until the liquid is absorbed. Fluff up the rice with a fork and leave off the heat, uncovered.

Chop the onions, garlic, celery and pepper finely. Heat the oil and butter in a large flameproof casserole, or large, heavy-based frying pan. Add the onions and garlic and cook until translucent. Add the tomatoes with their juice and the tomato purée and stir together for a few minutes. Next add the celery, pepper, 1 tablespoon (15 ml spoon) of the parsley, the cloves, thyme, cayenne pepper, the remaining teaspoon (5 ml spoon) of salt and some black pepper. Simmer gently, covered, for 15 minutes. Add the ham and prawns and when they are heated through add the partly cooked rice. Stir together over a moderate heat until the rice has absorbed the liquid in the pan. Serve at once, garnished with the remaining parsley.

YANKEE POT ROAST

oz (25 g) plain flour

–5 lb (1.8–2.25 kg) rolled
ibs, topside or brisket of
eef

oz (25 g) dripping or
tablespoons (2 × 15 ml
poon) oil

/2 pint (300 ml) beef stock

small carrots, chopped

medium-size onions,
hopped

small sticks of celery,
hopped

/2 bay leaf

few parsley stalks

/2 teaspoon (2.5 ml spoon)
hyme

tablespoon (15 ml spoon)
rrowroot or cornflour

tablespoons (2 × 15 ml
poon) cold water

alt and pepper

**Oven temperature
optional):**
Gas Mark 3/325°F/170°C

*The origin of the name 'Yankee' is uncertain but it is
thought to have been given to the early English settlers
by the Indians. Before ovens were commonplace, pot
roasting over heat was the usual way of braising meat.
Whether cooked in the oven or on a stove, pot roasting
is a delicious way of tenderising inexpensive cuts of
meat like brisket. This dish tastes even better the next
day, sliced thinly and reheated in the sauce. It goes
well with noodles or boiled potatoes.*

Preheat the oven. Season the flour with salt and
pepper and place on a piece of greaseproof paper.
Dry the meat with kitchen towelling and roll in
the seasoned flour. Heat the fat in a frying pan,
or a flameproof casserole large enough to hold
the beef, and brown the beef on all sides. Pour
out the fat and add the stock, vegetables, herbs
and more salt and pepper. Bring to the boil and
then transfer to a casserole dish if necessary.
Cover with a close-fitting lid, place in the centre
of the preheated oven and cook for 3–4 hours.
Alternatively, simmer very gently, allowing 35
minutes per 1 lb (450 g) plus an extra 20 minutes.
When a sharp-pronged fork can pierce the
middle of the joint with comparative ease it is
cooked. Remove the meat to a heated platter and
keep warm in a low oven while you make the
sauce.

Strain the contents of the pan through a sieve
into a saucepan, pressing the juices out of the
braising vegetables. (Discard the vegetables or
save them for making soup.) Bring the liquid to
a simmer and skim off any fat that rises to the
surface. Blend the arrowroot or cornflour with
the water and add it to the liquid. Simmer for a
few minutes and taste for seasoning. Serve in a
sauceboat to accompany the sliced meat.

17

BURRITOS

Basic recipe: Chilli con Carne, page 38

For the crêpes:

4 oz (100 g) plain flour

¼ teaspoon (1.25 ml spoon) salt

3 eggs

a scant ½ pint (300 ml) milk

1 oz (25 g) butter, melted

2 oz (50 g) melted butter or oil for frying

For the sauce:

½ pint (300 ml) milk

½ bay leaf

½ oz (15 g) butter

1 tablespoon (15 ml spoon) plain flour

2 oz (50 g) freshly grated parmesan or mature Cheddar cheese

1 teaspoon (5 ml spoon) Dijon mustard

salt and pepper

For the filling:

1 quantity of Chilli con Carne

To serve:

shredded lettuce, chopped onions, grated cheese

Oven temperature:
Gas Mark 6/400°F/200°C

These Mexican-inspired crêpes are filled with a spicy meat chilli and baked in a creamy cheese sauce. They are a favourite in our household. As the filling is the Chilli con Carne recipe, I make the latter in large quantities and freeze some to have on hand for Burritos.

To make the crêpes, sift the flour with the salt into a bowl. Make a well in the centre and add half the milk. Whisk the milk into the flour gradually and then whisk in the eggs, one at a time. Add the melted butter and half the remaining milk – do not over-mix. Leave the batter for at least 1 hour.

Just before using the batter, stir in enough of the remaining milk to bring it to the consistency of thin single cream. Heat a large, heavy frying pan and brush with a thin layer of the melted butter or oil. Add two-thirds of a soup ladle of batter to the pan and tilt quickly so that the bottom is covered. The crêpes should be about 8 inches (20 cm) across. Pour off any excess batter. Cook over a medium-high heat until browned; then turn the crêpe over and cook the other side. Turn out on to a plate and continue with the rest of the batter, piling the cooked crêpes on top of one another. Grease the pan whenever the crêpes start to stick.

If you wish to freeze the crêpes for later use, place greaseproof paper between them to separate.

To make the sauce, bring the milk and bay leaf to just below boiling point. Meanwhile, melt the butter in another pan and whisk in the flour. Cook together for a few minutes, take off the heat and whisk in the hot milk. Season with salt and pepper and simmer for 5 minutes. Remove from the heat and add the grated cheese and mustard. Preheat the oven.

To assemble the Burritos, place 2 heaped tablespoons (3–4 × 15 ml spoon) of Chilli con Carne on each crêpe. Roll them up and place seam side down in a greased ovenproof dish. Cover with the sauce and bake in the preheated oven for about 20 minutes. Serve with additional grated cheese, chopped onions and shredded lettuce.

JEWISH-STYLE CORNED BEEF

Makes sufficient for approx. 14 sandwiches

6 pints (3.5 litres) water

1 lb (450 g) sea salt

3 oz (75 g) brown sugar

2 heaped tablespoons (3–4 × 15 ml spoon) pickling spices

1/2 oz (15 g) saltpetre (available at chemists) – optional

4 bay leaves

4 1/2–5 lb (2–2.25 kg) piece of brisket of beef

7 cloves of garlic, peeled

2 onions, peeled and quartered

2 sticks of celery

New York City delicatessens are noted for their Jewish-style corned beef sandwiches and it is one of the first things I have when I go back there. The corned beef is sliced while hot and served between rye bread with mustard and dill pickles on the side. I was delighted to find that I could produce the same thing so easily at home. The brisket needs to stay in the brine for 12 days, and so you have to plan ahead, but it is well worth the wait. Serve it in sandwiches at a large lunch gathering or use it as you would any cold meat.

To prepare the brine, combine the water, salt, sugar, pickling spices, saltpetre and bay leaves and boil together in a very large saucepan for 5 minutes. Remove from the heat and cool.

Place the beef with the garlic in a stoneware or enamelled casserole and pour in the brine. Weigh down the beef with a heavy board so that it is immersed in the brine and cover the casserole. Set aside in a cool place for 12 days.

Remove the meat from the brine and wash it under cold running water. Place it in a large pan, cover with cold water and bring to the boil. Pour off the water and add fresh cold water, together with the onions and celery. Bring this to the boil and simmer over a very low heat, partially covered, for 4 hours, or until the meat is tender when pierced with a knife. Slice thinly while still warm and serve between soft rye bread.

SOUTHERN FRIED CHICKEN

2½ lb (1.25 kg) chicken pieces

2 oz (50 g) plain flour

1 tablespoon (15 ml spoon) salt

4 oz (100 g) butter

8 tablespoons (8 × 15 ml spoon) sunflower oil

For the cream gravy:

1 tablespoon (15 ml spoon) arrowroot or cornflour

¼ pint (150 ml) chicken stock

¼ pint (150 ml) single cream

salt and freshly ground black pepper

This version of Southern Fried Chicken is delicious enough to grace a dinner party. The chicken is sautéed in butter and oil, which makes the skin brown and crunchy and gives it a wonderful flavour. Even the most finicky child will want 'seconds'. The cream gravy is the traditional accompaniment but I love it just with a squeeze of lemon.

Dry the chicken pieces with kitchen towelling. Mix the flour and salt, put in a strong paper bag and shake a few pieces of chicken in the bag to coat evenly with the seasoned flour. Continue until all the pieces are floured.

Heat the butter and oil in a large frying pan that can easily hold all the pieces in one layer, or use a smaller pan and do half at a time. When the fat is very hot and beginning to bubble, add the chicken pieces, skin side down, starting with the thighs and legs to allow them a longer cooking time. When they are brown on one side turn them and brown the other side. Reduce the heat, cover the pan and continue cooking until the pieces are done, about 15 minutes. Remove the chicken from the pan and keep warm in a low oven.

To make the gravy, pour off all but 2 tablespoons (2 × 15 ml spoon) of the fat from the pan (this can be strained and used again). Stir in the arrowroot or cornflour and then the stock and cream. Cook for a few minutes, stirring with a whisk, until the gravy is thick. Season with salt and pepper and serve in a gravy boat to pour over the chicken.

Southern Fried Chicken with Cajun Potato Salad

CAJUN POTATO SALAD

Serves 6

2 lb (900 g) new potatoes

¼ pint (150 ml) dry white wine, or a mixture of half dry vermouth and half chicken stock

1 tablespoon (15 ml spoon) wine vinegar

1 tablespoon (15 ml spoon) lemon juice

1 teaspoon (5 ml spoon) Dijon mustard

5 tablespoons (5 × 15 ml spoon) olive oil

4–6 tablespoons (4–6 × 15 ml spoon) finely chopped spring onions or shallots

salt and freshly ground black pepper

Louisiana cuisine acquired its Gallic flavour from the Cajuns, descendants of the Acadians, the displaced French settlers of Nova Scotia. You can taste the French influence in this delicious potato salad. When it is made carefully it is quite special. Do not be tempted to use yesterday's cold boiled potatoes!

Wash the potatoes and put them in enough boiling, salted water to cover. Boil until the potatoes are just tender when pierced with a small knife. Drain and, when they are cool enough to handle, peel and cut into thin slices. Place the still-warm potatoes in a bowl and pour over the wine or vermouth and stock.

Mix together the vinegar, lemon juice, mustard and ¼ teaspoon (1.25 ml spoon) salt. Beat in the oil, drop by drop, and season to taste with pepper and more salt if needed. Pour this dressing over the potatoes, add the spring onions or shallots and toss gently to blend.

SUCCOTASH

Serves 4–6 as an accompaniment

¼ pint (150 ml) water

1 teaspoon (5 ml spoon) salt

1 teaspoon (5 ml spoon) sugar

8 oz (225 g) broad beans, fresh or frozen

9 oz (250 g) sweet corn, fresh or frozen

a knob of butter

5 fl oz (150 ml) carton of double cream

freshly ground black pepper

Succotash is an Indian word for a dish that contains both corn and beans. I use broad beans and corn in this tasty version.

Bring the water with the salt and sugar to the boil. Add the beans and corn, fresh or still frozen, to the pan and simmer for about 10 minutes, or until the beans are just tender. Drain and add the butter, cream and some pepper. Stir over a moderate heat until the cream and vegetables are very hot. Serve at once.

CHICKEN TAMALE PIE

Serves 4

3 lb (1.3 kg) chicken, cut into serving pieces

1 stick of celery with the leaves

1 few parsley stalks

1/2 bay leaf

1 oz (25 g) butter

1 tablespoon (15 ml spoon) sunflower oil

1 small onion, chopped finely

1 clove of garlic, chopped finely

1/2–1 teaspoon (2.5–5 ml spoon) chilli powder

1 teaspoon (5 ml spoon) dried oregano

14 oz (397 g) can of chopped tomatoes

8 oz (225 g) frozen corn kernels

4 oz (100 g) cornmeal (polenta)

2 oz (50 g) freshly grated parmesan or mature Cheddar cheese

salt and pepper

Oven temperature:
Gas Mark 4/350°F/180°C

In Texas and Mexico tamales are attractively wrapped in corn husks and steamed but this pan version is equally good. This tamale pie is a blend of tender chicken, with a spicy tomato and corn sauce snugly cooked in a cornmeal nest. The contrast of texture, flavour and colour is unusual and very tasty. Serve with a simple green salad.

Place the chicken pieces, celery, parsley and bay leaf in a large saucepan and just cover with water. Bring to the boil and simmer gently, covered, for 25 minutes, or until the chicken is tender. Drain the chicken, reserving the broth. When it is cool enough to handle, remove all the meat from the bones. (Save the bones to add to the leftover broth, to make some more chicken stock later for other recipes.)

While the chicken is cooking, heat the butter and oil in a saucepan and gently cook the onion and garlic until translucent. Stir in the chilli powder and oregano and then add the tomatoes. Simmer for 15 minutes before adding the corn kernels and then cook for a further 5 minutes. Season well with salt and pepper and put aside.

Measure out ¾ pint (450 ml) of the broth and season well with salt and pepper. Pour into a saucepan and bring to the boil. Slowly pour in the cornmeal, whisking all the time, and continue to whisk until it becomes very thick, like mashed potatoes. This will take about 5–10 minutes.

Preheat the oven. Lightly grease a large casserole dish and line the bottom and sides with the cornmeal. Spread the chicken over the cornmeal and season with salt and pepper. Cover with the tomato and corn mixture and then the cheese. Bake for 30 minutes and serve from the casserole.

LOUISIANA FISH FILLET PARCELS

½ pint (300 ml) shrimps

1 small carrot

1 small stick of celery

2 shallots, minced very finely

2 tablespoons (2 × 15 ml spoon) butter

a pinch of cayenne pepper

2 tablespoons (2 × 15 ml spoon) plain flour

2 tablespoons (2 × 15 ml spoon) white wine

4 tablespoons (4 × 15 ml spoon) double cream

1 tablespoon (15 ml spoon) parsley, chopped very finely

4 × 8 oz (225 g) fillet of plaice or sole

salt

Oven temperature:
Gas Mark 7/425°F/220°C

In 1901 Antoine's Restaurant in New Orleans honoured the balloonist Alberto Santos-Dumont by creating this now-famous dish of fish and creamy seafood sauce baked in balloon-shaped envelopes. What an inspiration it was! It is always an exciting moment when guests open their own surprise parcel and taste the contents. I often cook whole fish, stuffed with herbs, in paper parcels like this.

Peel the shrimps, removing the heads and the shells and put all the peelings in a saucepan with the carrot and celery and ½ pint (300 ml) water. Cover and simmer for 20 minutes.

In another saucepan, gently sauté the shallots in the butter until translucent. Add the cayenne pepper and cook for a few seconds before stirring in the flour. Whisk the strained shrimp stock and wine into the pan until the sauce thickens. Add the cream, parsley, shrimps and seasoning. Preheat the oven.

Cut out four heart shapes from four 15-inch (38 cm) squares of greaseproof paper. Fold them in half, place a fish fillet, generously covered with sauce, on one side. Fold the other side over and roll and crimp the edges at ½-inch (1 cm) intervals to seal the fish in. Place the envelopes on a baking sheet and bake for 15–20 minutes. Serve at once on individual warmed plates with, for instance, boiled potatoes and courgettes.

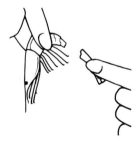

Louisiana Fish Fillet Parcels

WESTERN PORK SPARE-RIBS

4½ lb (2 kg) pork ribs

salt

For the sauce:

2 medium-size onions, chopped finely

2 oz (50 g) soft brown sugar

6 tablespoons (6 × 15 ml spoon) cider vinegar

½ pint (300 ml) tomato ketchup

3–4 tablespoons (3–4 × 15 ml spoon) Worcestershire sauce

1 teaspoon (5 ml spoon) dry mustard

a dash of Tabasco sauce

salt and freshly ground black pepper

Oven temperatures:
Gas Mark 6/400°F/200°C
Gas Mark 4/350°F/180°C

Spare-ribs of pork have been popular in America for a long time and happily they are now easy to find here. They can be cooked outdoors and basted with the sauce or done in the oven, which is often more convenient. The sweet–sour sauce coats the ribs with a dark shiny glaze and gives the meat a spicy flavour. The best way to eat them is with your fingers – messy but delicious. Allow at least 12 oz (350 g) meat per person, as there is a lot of bone. Serve with rice and a green vegetable, such as cabbage or brussels sprouts.

Preheat the oven to the higher setting. Cut between the flesh of the ribs to make individual pieces. Place in a shallow roasting tin, sprinkle with salt and roast for 15 minutes.

Meanwhile, prepare the sauce. Combine all the ingredients in a saucepan and simmer for 5 minutes.

Lower the oven to the second setting. Pour away any fat from the roasting pan. Cover the ribs with the sauce and continue to bake for another 45 minutes, basting from time to time with the sauce. Serve the ribs with the sauce spooned over.

BUTTERFLY LAMB

Serves 8–10

5½–6 lb (2.5–2.7 kg) leg of lamb, boned (see below)

5 tablespoons (5 × 15 ml spoon) olive oil

5 tablespoons (5 × 15 ml spoon) soy sauce

2 cloves of garlic, chopped finely

1 tablespoon (15 ml spoon) dried thyme

salt and freshly ground black pepper

Oven temperature (optional):
Gas Mark 5/375°F/190°C

In the past few years this has been an American favourite for barbecues. It has the added advantage of being excellent for roasting – ideal for this country with its succulent lamb and uncertain weather. It is a dream to slice and serve, let alone eat!

The leg of lamb should be boned but still in one piece, so that it can be laid out flat. The lobes of meat will be on either side of the thinner centre, making a butterfly shape.

Dry the meat with kitchen towelling. Combine the oil, soy sauce, garlic, thyme and pepper to make the marinade. Place the meat in a large shallow dish and pour over the marinade, turning the meat so that all the sides are coated. Cover the dish with cling film and leave for at least 2 hours but preferably overnight in a cool place. Before you cook the lamb, you can place 2 long skewers through the meat if you like to hold it flat and create a handle for turning.

To barbecue: allow the coals of a large fire to turn completely red before you begin. It is impossible to give an exact time because of the heat and distance of the fire, but allow about 35 minutes for lamb that is still rosy inside and crisp on the outside. Turn the lamb several times while it cooks and baste with the marinade or some oil. Allow the meat to rest on a warmed platter for a few minutes before carving.

To roast: preheat the oven. Roast the meat in the middle of the oven for about 25–30 minutes. If you have a grill, preheat it, brush the roasted meat with oil and grill the meat for a few minutes on either side to crisp the outside. If you do not grill, allow a further 10 minutes or so in the oven. Allow the meat to rest for several minutes on a heated platter before carving.

HAMBURGERS

Hamburgers should be made with a good, lean minced beef. Form the meat into patties of about 5–6 oz (150–175 g) lightly (too much handling makes the meat tough). Heat enough fat in a frying pan to cover the bottom, then sear the hamburgers over a high heat on both sides. Season with salt and pepper after the meat is seared and continue cooking, over a lower heat, turning once or twice until they are cooked to your taste. For outdoor grill cooking, sear the patties over a hot fire and then place them around the edges of the grill where the heat is less intense, to cook more slowly.

Serve them in soft hamburger rolls – Sainsbury's have some delicious sesame-seeded baps. If you like cheeseburgers, add a slice of Cheddar-type cheese on top of the hamburger for the last few minutes of cooking, or try some grated cheese mixed in with the meat. Slices of fresh onion and tomatoes or leaves of crunchy iceberg lettuce add a crisp bite to the burger. Add mayonnaise, ketchup, or mustard for a special flavour. Sainsbury's range of relishes – Cucumber, Tomato, Sweetcorn, Mild Mustard, Tomato and Chilli – may be served separately.

Hamburgers; Butterfly Lamb; Western Pork Spare-ribs

EGGS BENEDICT

Serves 4

For the hollandaise sauce:

3 egg yolks

2 tablespoons (2 × 15 ml spoon) fresh lemon juice

5 oz (150 g) butter

2 tablespoons (2 × 15 ml spoon) double cream (if needed – see method below)

salt and freshly ground black pepper

For the muffins:

4 muffins

butter for spreading

6 oz (175 g) sliced cooked ham

vinegar

8 eggs, new-laid if possible

Oven temperature:
lowest setting

Eggs Benedict are said to have been created by a New York chef as a restorative for a Mr Benedict's 'morning after'! They are very good for lunch or brunch, that combination of breakfast and lunch that is so popular on Sundays in America. The Americans invented a muffin which they called an 'English muffin' and the muffins now available here are very similar. They provide the perfect base for the ham and poached eggs covered in hollandaise sauce – a wonderful combination.

To make the sauce, place the egg yolks, lemon juice, salt and pepper in a liquidiser or food processor and whizz together for 15 seconds. In a small saucepan, melt the butter until it foams (but do not allow it to brown). Whizz the eggs again and pour in the bubbling butter in a very slow stream. The butter must be bubbling or the sauce will not thicken. Scrape the thickened sauce into the top of a double boiler, or into a bowl set over a pan of hot water, to keep warm while you prepare the rest of the dish. If it thickens too much, add the double cream. If it should curdle, whisk in 1 tablespoon (15 ml spoon) boiling water.

Heat the oven on its lowest setting. Split the muffins by piercing all around the sides with a fork and then pulling apart. Toast and butter the muffins, cover with a slice of ham and place them on a serving dish in the oven.

To poach the eggs, fill a shallow pan three-quarters full of water and add 1 tablespoon (15 ml spoon) of vinegar for every 2 pints (1.2 litres) of water. Bring the water to boiling point. Break each egg separately into a cup and slide it into the water. Insert a slotted spoon under the egg and carefully turn the white over the egg. Continue with the other eggs. You may have to do them in two batches. Poach for 3 minutes. Remove them with a slotted spoon and place them on a clean cloth. Trim away any ragged edges.

When the eggs are done, place them on the ham-covered muffins and cover with 3 tablespoons (3 × 15 ml spoon) of hollandaise sauce. Serve at once.

IMPROMPTU TUNA FISH CASSEROLE

Serves 4

2 oz (50 g) butter

1 green or red pepper, seeded and chopped

7 oz (198 g) can of tuna fish, drained and flaked

1 tablespoon (15 ml spoon) salt

8 oz (225 g) Chinese or other egg noodles

10½ oz (295 g) can of condensed cream of celery or mushroom soup

5 fl oz (150 ml) carton of single cream

½ teaspoon (2.5 ml spoon) curry powder (optional)

1 oz (25 g) fresh breadcrumbs

Oven temperature:
Gas Mark 7/425°F/220°C

This is one of those emergency dishes that Americans are so good at concocting. It is inexpensive and surprisingly tasty and good. The condensed soup becomes a creamy sauce for the noodles, pepper and tuna. Serve it with a green salad.

Gently heat 1 oz (25 g) of the butter in a small frying pan and sauté the pepper until it is soft. Remove from the heat and stir in the tuna. Preheat the oven.

Meanwhile, in a large saucepan, bring 4 pints (2.25 litres) water to the boil, add the salt and the noodles and boil briskly until the noodles are 'al dente' – with quite a bit of bite left in them. Drain the noodles, pour them into a greased ovenproof dish and toss with the remaining butter. Pour the tuna and pepper mixture over the noodles.

Empty the soup into a bowl and mix in the cream, and the curry powder if you are using it. Pour this soup mixture over the tuna and sprinkle with the breadcrumbs. Bake in the preheated oven for 15–20 minutes.

BAKED GLAZED GAMMON

Pictured on page 85

3–4 lb (1.3–1.8 kg)
gammon joint

dry cider (optional)

1 onion stuck with cloves,
1 bay leaf, 1 stick of celery
and a few black peppercorns
(all optional)

whole cloves for studding

For a honey glaze:

5 tablespoons (5 × 15 ml
spoon) honey

5 teaspoons (5 × 5 ml
spoon) mild, Dijon-type
mustard

For a brown sugar glaze:

5 oz (150 g) soft dark brown
sugar

1 teaspoon (5 ml spoon) dry
mustard

4 tablespoons (4 × 15 ml
spoon) milk

Oven temperature:
Gas Mark 6/400°F/200°C

In America, glazed hams are very popular. From the special Smithfield hams from Virginia to more everyday gammon, oven glazes are used to enhance the taste and presentation. They turn gammon into a festive dish. Served hot it goes well with scalloped potatoes and puréed spinach or broccoli, or you can serve cold slices with a variety of salads or home-made pickles (pages 83–86).

Soak the gammon overnight in cold water and then bring to the boil in fresh water. (Alternatively, cover the gammon in cold water and bring to the boil; repeat with fresh water, or half water, half cider.) Simmer gently, covered, allowing 25 minutes per lb (450 g). If you wish, add the onion stuck with cloves, bay leaf, celery and black peppercorns. Preheat the oven.

Allow the gammon to cool in the cooking water, and drain it. Strip off the skin with a sharp knife. Score the fat in squares and stud the corners with cloves. Bake the gammon in a greased shallow roasting tin, in the preheated oven for 20 minutes.

Meanwhile, mix together the ingredients for one glaze. Remove the gammon from the oven and brush the fat with the glaze. Replace and cook for a further 20 minutes, basting frequently with the glaze, until the gammon is golden.

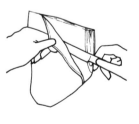  

Eggs Benedict (recipe on page 30)

VERMONT CHICKEN PIE

4 lb (1.8 kg) roasting chicken

2 sticks of celery, chopped

1 medium-size onion, sliced

sprigs of thyme, tarragon and parsley

1 bay leaf

1¾ pints (1 litre) water

1½ oz (40 g) butter

1½ oz (40 g) plain flour

salt and freshly ground black pepper

For the biscuits:

7 oz (200 g) strong white flour

a pinch of salt

3 teaspoons (3 × 5 ml spoon) baking powder

2½ oz (65 g) butter

¼ pint (150 ml) milk

2 tablespoons (2 × 15 ml spoon) chopped fresh herbs

Oven temperature:
Gas Mark 7/425°F/220°C

This is a chicken pie with a difference. Instead of a pastry lid this pie has a cover made from American-style baking powder biscuits. It looks as appetising as it tastes. It is a fine informal party dish, as it can be assembled in advance. Serve it with rosemary spinach (page 46) and creamed radishes (page 47) for a New England feast.

Place the chicken in a saucepan just large enough to hold it snugly. Add the celery, onion, herbs, salt and pepper. Pour in the water which should come about half-way up the chicken, leaving the breast dry. Cover the pan and simmer gently for 50 minutes. This will poach the brown meat and steam the white.

Remove the chicken from the pot and allow it to cool before removing and chopping the meat. Strain the cooking liquid and vegetables through a fine sieve, pressing down hard with the back of a spoon to extract as much juice and flavour as possible. Reserve 1 pint (600 ml) of the stock for the sauce. (The remaining stock can be poured over the chicken bones and simmered for another 40 minutes to make stock for another time.)

Heat the butter in a heavy saucepan, add the flour and whisk to form a smooth paste. Whisk in the reserved stock and continue to whisk until the sauce thickens. Leave it to simmer gently, uncovered, for 10 minutes. Add the chopped chicken to the sauce and taste for seasoning. Pour into a 3-pint (1.7-litre) gratin dish and cover with foil. Preheat the oven.

For the biscuits: sift the flour, salt and baking powder, cut in the butter and rub with your fingers until the mixture is crumb-like. Pour in the milk and herbs and stir with a spoon until a soft dough is formed. Roll the dough out on a floured surface and cut into 14 rounds, 2½ inch (6.5 cm) across and ¼ inch (5 mm) thick. Place these on a greased baking sheet.

Bake the chicken in the lower half of the oven and the biscuits in the top for about 15 minutes, until the biscuits are brown. The chicken may need another 5–10 minutes before it is bubbling and heated through. Remove the foil and cover the top of the pie with the hot biscuits, fitting them as closely as possible. Serve at once.

SISTER ABIGAIL'S BLUE FLOWER OMELETTE

Serves 1

2 eggs

a pinch of salt

1 tablespoon (15 ml spoon) unsalted butter

1 teaspoon (5 ml spoon) chopped fresh chives

6 chive flowers

The Shakers were a small religious faction from England. They arrived in 1774, nine strong, led by their prophetess Ann Lees. Their first American commune was established near Albany. There they withdrew from the sinful world and lived a life of celibacy. They engaged in dances during which they literally 'shook' to cast off evil. Their cuisine included the use of lots of spices and herbs and was an important influence in American cuisine. To live up to its name this Shaker recipe should be made when the chive plant flowers, but a well made omelette is always a delight even when plain.

Beat the eggs and salt with a fork, just enough to blend the whites and yolks thoroughly, about 30 seconds. Melt the butter over a high heat in an 8-inch (20 cm) frying pan (non-stick if possible). Tip the pan to spread the butter evenly over the bottom and sides. When the hot butter has almost stopped foaming, and is just about to colour, pour in the eggs. With the back of a fork start stirring the eggs quickly in a circular movement covering the bottom of the pan. At the same time shake the pan with your other hand. Almost instantly the eggs will begin to form soft liquid curds. While the eggs are still slightly liquid, and still using the back of the fork, spread the eggs out to fill any gaps. All of this should only take about 25 seconds. Add the chives and chive flowers, tilt the pan and slide the fork under the omelette near the handle. Fold the omelette over and slide on to a warm plate.

BOSTON BAKED BEANS

1 lb (450 g) dried haricot beans

1 oz (25 g) soft brown sugar

6 tablespoons (6 × 15 ml spoon) black treacle

1 tablespoon (15 ml spoon) dry mustard

1 teaspoon (5 ml spoon) salt

½ teaspoon (2.5 ml spoon) black pepper

4 cloves

2 small onions

12 oz (350 g) piece of streaky bacon, with the rind removed

3–4 fl oz (80–110 ml) rum (optional)

Oven temperature:
Gas Mark 1/275°F/140°C

In Puritan Boston no work was done on the Sabbath, which lasted from sundown on Saturday until sundown on Sunday. Women cooked their Sunday meal of baked beans the day before in the slow heat of a fireplace or took the family bean pot to the local baker who would return it with some Boston Brown Bread (page 56) in time for the Sabbath. Home-made baked beans are a very special treat.

Cover the beans with cold water and leave to soak overnight. In the morning put the beans and soaking water in a saucepan and add more water to cover the beans by 1 inch (2.5 cm). Boil rapidly for at least 15 minutes. Cover and simmer the beans gently until tender, about 1 hour. Drain the beans, reserving the water, into a very large casserole.

Preheat the oven. Combine the sugar, treacle, mustard, salt and pepper and stir into the beans. Stick 2 cloves into each onion and mix into the beans. Score the bacon fat and push the bacon into the beans. Add the reserved water and enough extra water to cover the beans.

Cover the casserole and bake in the preheated oven for at least 4 hours. Check occasionally to see if it is dry and add more water if necessary. Remove the cover for the last 45 minutes of cooking time. Add the rum, if used, and bring the bacon to the surface, so that the fat can become brown. Serve the beans from the casserole with a slice of bacon for each serving.

*Boston Baked Beans;
Chilli Con Carne*

CHILLI CON CARNE

1½ lb (675 g) lean stewing beef, cut into strips 3 inches (7 cm) long and ¼ inch (5 mm) wide

3 tablespoons (3 × 15 ml spoon) sunflower oil

2 medium-size onions, chopped

2 cloves of garlic, chopped

2 teaspoons (2 × 5 ml spoon) chilli powder

½ teaspoon (2.5 ml spoon) dried oregano

½ teaspoon (2.5 ml spoon) ground cumin

14 oz (397 g) can of chopped tomatoes

¼ pint (150 ml) water

15½ oz (439 g) can of red kidney or pinto beans

salt and pepper

Originally from Texas and Mexico, Chilli con Carne is now eaten throughout the United States, no doubt because it is such a tasty economical dish and can be 'stretched' by adding more beans. With long, slow simmering the beef and beans turn into a fragrant, brown, spicy stew, always popular with the young. It goes well with a green salad.

Pat the meat dry with kitchen towelling. Heat 2 tablespoons (2 × 15 ml spoon) of the oil in a frying pan and brown the meat in two batches. Transfer the meat to a heavy saucepan.

Add the remaining tablespoon (15 ml spoon) of oil to the frying pan and cook the onions and garlic for a few minutes, stirring frequently. Stir in the chilli powder, oregano and cumin and cook for a further few minutes. Add the tomatoes and water and stir together, scraping up any bits from the bottom, before adding to the meat in the saucepan. Season well with salt and pepper, cover and cook at a low simmer for 3 hours. Check occasionally to make sure that it is not sticking and add a little water if necessary.

Drain the beans, add them to the pan and cook until heated through (about 15 minutes). Taste and correct the seasoning before serving. This dish can be cooked and kept in the refrigerator for 3 days. Reheat thoroughly for at least 20 minutes before serving.

Notes: chilli powders and chilli seasonings vary in strength. Begin with 2 teaspoons (2 × 5 ml spoon) chilli powder, as given above, and add more later, after tasting, if you want a hotter chilli flavour. This recipe can be varied by using half minced beef and half stewing beef for the meat ingredient.

AMERICAN MEATLOAF

1 medium-size onion,
chopped finely

1 oz (25 g) butter

2 lb (900 g) lean minced beef

1 lb (450 g) minced pork, or
a combination of minced
pork and veal

3 eggs

3 oz (75 g) fresh
breadcrumbs

2 oz (50 g) fresh parsley,
chopped finely

2 tablespoons (2 × 15 ml
spoon) chopped fresh chives
or spring onion tops
(optional)

2 teaspoons (2 × 5 ml
spoon) Worcestershire sauce

2 teaspoons (2 × 5 ml
spoon) salt

freshly ground black pepper

8 rashers of thin, rindless,
streaky bacon

Oven temperature:
Gas Mark 4 / 350°F / 180°C

*Meatloaf really needs no introduction and I only
include my favourite way of making it because an
American cookbook would not be complete without a
recipe for one. What a useful dish it is! Inexpensive
and adaptable, it goes well with all kinds of vegetables
and is delicious sliced cold, in sandwiches with
mayonnaise or served with a salad. This meatloaf is
moist and tasty yet slices well hot or cold.*

Preheat the oven. In a small frying pan, sauté the
onion in the butter until translucent. Mix it with
all the other ingredients, except the bacon, in a
large mixing bowl. Transfer the mixture to a
greased roasting pan and lightly pat it into a loaf
about 12 inches (30 cm) long, 5 inches (13 cm)
wide and 3 inches (8 cm) high. Cover with the
bacon rashers and bake in the preheated oven for
1½ hours.

   If serving hot, serve with a favourite home-
made tomato sauce or a sauce made from soured
cream with a little mustard added.

CANDIED SWEET POTATOES

Serves 4–6

2 lb (900 g) sweet potatoes

4 oz (100 g) soft brown sugar or 4 fl oz (110 ml) maple syrup

½ teaspoon (2.5 ml spoon) grated lemon rind

juice of ½ small lemon

2 oz (50 g) butter

salt

Oven temperature:
Gas Mark 5/375°F/190°C

Sweet potatoes are frequently served at Thanksgiving and they are a delicious accompaniment to ham and pork, as well as poultry. They were introduced to Europe by Columbus in 1493 and were soon known as Spanish potatoes. In Tudor England they were enjoyed in the form of crystallised slices. They are delicious baked in their jackets like ordinary potatoes but they are particularly appetising candied, when they come out of the oven a lovely glazed orange colour.

Cook the sweet potatoes in their skins in boiling, salted water until nearly tender, about 20 minutes. Drain, peel and cut into ½-inch (1 cm) slices. Place in a greased, large, shallow baking dish and sprinkle with salt, followed by the sugar or maple syrup and the lemon rind and juice. Dot with the butter and bake uncovered in the preheated oven for 20–25 minutes, basting occasionally with the syrup. Pour the syrup over the potatoes when serving.

CREAMED ONIONS

Serves 4–6

2 lb (900 g) small pickling onions, peeled

½ pint (300 ml) water

1 pint (600 ml) milk

½ bay leaf

1 oz (25 g) butter

2 tablespoons (2 × 15 ml spoon) plain flour

salt and freshly ground white pepper

To garnish:

chopped parsley or coriander leaves

Early American settlers found onions to be a native crop and used them to enhance many dishes. Creamed onions are as traditional as turkey at Thanksgiving dinner and a lovely vegetable to have at any time. Small pickling onions are just right for this dish. If you peel them in cold water you avoid stinging eyes.

Place the peeled onions in a medium-size saucepan with the water and a good pinch of salt. Cover and simmer gently until the onions are tender when pierced with a knife but still retain their shape – about 20 minutes. Drain them and put aside.

In a small saucepan, heat the milk and the bay leaf to just below a simmer. Melt the butter in a heavy saucepan and when it bubbles (do not allow it to brown) add the flour and cook for a few minutes. Remove from the heat and whisk in the milk gradually. Return to the heat and cook, uncovered, very gently until thickened. Remove the bay leaf and season well with salt and pepper. Add the onions and cook together until the onions are well heated. Pour into a hot serving dish and garnish with the parsley or coriander.

SPOON BREAD

Serves 3–4 as a main dish

½ *pint (300 ml) milk*

1½ *oz (40 g) cornmeal (polenta)*

1 *oz (25 g) freshly grated parmesan or mature Cheddar cheese*

3 *eggs*

salt and cayenne pepper

Oven temperature:
Gas Mark 5/375°F/190°C

Spoon bread is a famous cornmeal dish from the South. Its origins can be traced to the Indian porridge known as suppawn. This light soufflé version makes an unusual and delicious luncheon dish. Serve it followed by Pecan Pie (page 67) for a taste of the South.

Preheat the oven. Grease a 3-pint (1.7-litre) soufflé dish. Put the milk in a pan and bring to just below boiling; then whisk the milk while slowly pouring in the cornmeal. Continue to whisk until the mixture has the consistency of very thick cream. Remove from the heat and stir in the cheese, salt and cayenne pepper.

Separate the eggs, one at a time, dropping the whites into a clean bowl and whisking the yolks into the corn mixture. Whisk the whites with a pinch of salt until stiff. Using a large metal spoon, first mix a heaped spoon of whites into the cornmeal mixture and then gently fold in the rest of the whites. Pour into the prepared dish and bake for 25–30 minutes until puffed and brown but still very soft inside. Serve at once.

RED FLANNEL HASH

4 oz (100 g) streaky bacon, with the rind removed

1 medium-size onion, chopped finely

1 lb (450 g) potatoes, boiled and chopped coarsely

1 lb (450 g) corned beef, home-made (page 19) or canned, chopped

8 oz (225 g) cooked beetroot, diced (not in vinegar)

5 tablespoons (5 × 15 ml spoon) double cream

4 tablespoons (4 × 15 ml spoon) parsley, chopped very finely

extra bacon fat if necessary

salt and freshly ground black pepper

Across America leftover corned beef is turned into delicious hash and has been a favourite breakfast or luncheon dish for generations. In New England Red Flannel Hash is popular and is named for its beetroot colouring, which is similar to the much used and loved red flannel material. Serve with poached eggs for a hearty breakfast or lunch.

In a heavy, large (10–12 inch/25–30 cm) frying pan, fry the bacon until crisp and brown. Remove it with a slotted spoon on to kitchen towelling. Pour off all but 2 tablespoons (2 × 15 ml spoon) fat from the frying pan and reserve. Add the onion to the pan and cook until it is translucent, about 5 minutes. Put in a large bowl. Chop the bacon roughly and add it to the onion. Mix in the potatoes, corned beef, beetroot, cream and half the parsley. Season with salt and pepper.

Measure 5 tablespoons (5 × 15 ml spoon) of the reserved fat (use extra fat if there is not enough) into the frying pan and heat it until it begins to bubble. Add the hash, spreading it evenly with a spatula. Cook over a low heat for about 40 minutes, shaking the pan occasionally to prevent sticking. When the bottom is golden brown, loosen around the edge with a spatula and turn upside-down on to a heated serving dish. Sprinkle the top with the remaining parsley and serve at once, topped with poached eggs if you wish.

HASH BROWN POTATOES

1½ lb (675 g) potatoes

½ oz (15 g) butter

4 oz (100 g) tendersweet bacon – English smoked streaky, rindless, extra-thin rashers

salt and freshly ground black pepper

Hash Brown Potatoes are served in many roadside cafés with eggs or hamburgers. The crispy brown covering with the soft potatoes underneath is absolutely delicious and makes a welcome change from french fries. You can use diced boiled potatoes but the grated potatoes are even nicer.

Peel and then coarsely grate the potatoes. Place them in a sieve and press them down with a large spoon or your hand to extract some of the liquid. Leave to drain.

Melt the butter in a large (approximately 11-inch/28 cm), heavy frying pan. Add the bacon and fry it until it is crisp and brown. Remove with a slotted spoon to kitchen towelling to drain. Add the grated potatoes to the fat in the pan and press them down evenly with a spatula to about a 1-inch (2 cm) thickness. Sprinkle liberally with salt and pepper and cook, covered, over a low heat for about 15 minutes. Uncover, raise the heat and cook a further 5 minutes, or until a brown crust forms on the bottom. Slip a spatula underneath to ease any bits that might be sticking. Turn over on to a heated dish. Crumble up the bacon, sprinkle over and serve immediately.

PENNSYLVANIA DUTCH-FRIED TOMATOES

This is a wonderful way to use up green tomatoes and improve the flavour of red hot-house ones. Green tomatoes that are almost about to go red or very firm red ones are best for this dish. This is the recipe as given to me by my American friend, Phil.

Slice the tomatoes into ½-inch (1 cm) rounds. Dip both sides in flour and fry in very hot fat, preferably dripping. When nearly black, turn over and sprinkle with salt and pepper and a good quantity of sugar. When the second side is almost black, pour over milk to half the depth of the tomatoes and boil briskly for 2–3 minutes. Serve the tomatoes on rounds of toast with the sauce poured over.

Red Flannel Hash; Pennsylvania Dutch-fried Tomatoes;
Hash Brown Potatoes

NEW POTATOES AND PEAS

Serves 6–8

3 lb (1.3 kg) very small new potatoes

4 oz (100 g) thin streaky bacon rashers

8–10 oz (225–275 g) fresh shelled peas

½ pint (300 ml) double cream

2 oz (50 g) butter, softened

fresh chives or parsley, chopped finely

salt and freshly ground black pepper

An American friend who was brought up on a farm outside Boston remembered her Aunt Hazel making this dish and how good it was.

Wash the potatoes but do not peel them. Steam them in a colander over a pan of boiling water until tender.

Meanwhile, fry the bacon until very crisp, drain on kitchen paper towelling and keep warm in a low oven. Put the peas and cream in a pan and cook until just tender, about 5 minutes. Combine the peas and potatoes in a warm serving dish. Break open some of the potatoes with a fork and spread with the butter and herbs. Season well with salt and pepper and gently toss together. Crumble up the bacon and sprinkle over the top. Serve immediately.

SPINACH WITH ROSEMARY SHAKER-STYLE

Serves 4

2 lb (900 g) fresh spinach

4–5 spring onions, bulbs and stems, chopped

1 teaspoon (5 ml spoon) finely chopped fresh rosemary

2 tablespoons (2 × 15 ml spoon) finely chopped fresh parsley

2 oz (50 g) butter

salt and freshly ground black pepper

One of the Shakers' main industries was the growing of herbs for medicinal use. A Shaker catalogue of the 1830s offered 354 kinds of medicinal plants, barks, roots, seeds and flowers. This led quite naturally to a widespread use of herbs in their cooking. This is their excellent way with spinach.

Wash the spinach in several changes of cold water. Place in a heavy saucepan, cover tightly and cook over a moderate heat for about 8 minutes. Turn into a colander and press to remove the surplus liquid. When it cools down, chop it fairly finely. Heat the butter in a saucepan and add the spring onions, rosemary and parsley. Add the spinach and stir over a brisk heat to mix in the herbs and reheat. Season well with salt and pepper and serve.

CREAMED RADISHES

Serves 4

2 bunches of radishes
(approx. 8 oz/225 g)

4 fl oz (110 ml) single
cream

salt and freshly ground black
pepper

This is another lovely Shaker idea. The radishes retain their crisp texture but take on a new dimension when they are simmered in cream.

Thinly slice the radishes. Place in a small saucepan with the cream and simmer very gently, covered, for about 8–10 minutes. The cream may look as if it has curdled but a few stirs will make it smooth again. Season with salt and pepper and serve.

CORN FRITTERS

Serves 6 as an accompaniment

4 ears of corn on the cob,
very fresh and young if
possible

2 eggs, separated

3 tablespoons (3 × 15 ml
spoon) plain flour

a good pinch of salt

2 tablespoons (2 × 15 ml
spoon) each butter and
vegetable oil, plus more
if required

When you bite through the crisp outside and taste the creamy centre of these delectable small pancakes you will understand why they are also known as corn oysters. Serve them with chicken or ham as a very special treat.

Remove the husks and silk from the ears. With a sharp knife, cut down the centre of each row of kernels. Place an ear upright in a large bowl and scrape down the ear with the back of the knife to push the creamy centre out of the kernels. Repeat with the other ears. You will end up with a slushy, creamy mixture.

Mix the egg yolks and then the flour into the mixture. Whisk the egg whites with a pinch of salt until stiff and fold into the corn mixture. Taste for seasoning. Using a heavy, large frying pan, heat the butter and oil until hot and foaming. Drop tablespoons (15 ml spoons) of the corn mixture into the hot fat and fry until the bottoms are crisp and brown. Turn them over and brown the other sides. Add more butter and oil to the pan as necessary. Keep the cooked fritters in a warm oven while making the rest.

AMERICAN BAKES AND DESSERTS

AMERICAN-STYLE BREAD AND ROLLS

Makes 2 lb (900 g) loaf or 18 rolls

1 lb (450 g) strong white flour (preferably unbleached) or a mixture of two-thirds strong white and one-third 100% wholemeal flour

2 teaspoons (2 × 5 ml spoon) salt

1 tablespoon (15 ml spoon) sugar

½ oz (15 g) fresh yeast or ¼ oz (7 g) dried yeast

½ pint (300 ml) lukewarm water

Oven temperatures:

For the loaf:

Gas Mark 6/400°F/200°C

For the rolls:

Gas Mark 7/425°F/220°C

There is nothing like the taste and smell of home-baked bread or rolls. A yeast dough is very adaptable and you can fit it in to suit your own timetable. So don't be put off by the time or temperature needed to allow a yeast dough to rise. A cool place, even the refrigerator, will slow down the process and you can be out all day and still bake a delicious loaf when you return. Even if you find the dough has collapsed from being left too long, knead it again and it will rise once more. Pretty-shaped home-baked rolls are easy to produce and always popular. Follow the directions for the basic recipe and shape it into one of the types of rolls below. The rolls can be reheated briefly just before serving if you make them in advance.

Place the flour and salt in a large bowl and put in a very low oven for about 5 minutes, to warm the flour slightly. Meanwhile, add the sugar and yeast to the lukewarm water and leave until the yeast is dissolved and starting to bubble (5–10 minutes).

Pour the yeast mixture into the flour and stir with a spoon, and then with your hand, until the dough comes away from the sides of the bowl. If it is too sticky add more flour, if too dry add a little warm water. Knead on a lightly floured surface until the dough is smooth and elastic. Put back in the bowl, cover with a plastic bag, and leave in a warm place (70–80°F/21–25°C) until doubled in volume (about 2–3 hours, depending on the temperature). The dough is now ready to be punched down and shaped before its final rising.

For a basic loaf: punch down the dough, shape into a rectangle and put in a greased 2 lb (1 kg) loaf tin. Place a plastic bag over the tin and leave

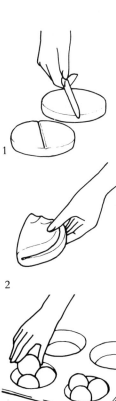

1

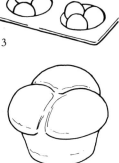

2

3

4

to rise again, until the dough is well above the top of the tin (1–2 hours). Bake in the centre of a preheated oven for 50 minutes. Turn the loaf out on to a wire rack to cool.

For Parker House Rolls: punch down and roll out to a ¼-inch (5 mm) thickness. Cut into 3–4-inch (8–10 cm) rounds. Brush each circle with melted butter. Make a crease across the circle to one side of the centre with the blunt side of a knife (1). Fold the smaller side of the circle over the larger and pinch the edges together (2). Place them, well spaced out, on a greased baking sheet and allow them to rise in a warm place until doubled in size. Bake in a preheated oven for about 20 minutes.

For Clover Leaf Rolls: punch down the dough. Then pinch off small pieces and shape them into 1½-inch (4 cm) balls by rolling them between your palms. Place 3 balls in each well of a greased bun tin (3) and put in a warm place (70–80°F/21–25°C) until doubled in size. Bake as for Parker House Rolls. The finished rolls resemble miniature cottage loaves (4).

For Crescent Rolls: punch down the dough and roll it out to a ½-inch (1 cm) thickness. Cut it into 12-inch (30 cm) circles. Brush the surface lightly with melted butter. Cut each circle into 8 wedges (5) and, starting at the outside, roll each wedge towards its point (6). Shape into crescents (7) and place them, well spaced out, on a greased baking sheet. Allow them to rise in a warm place until doubled in size. Bake as for Parker House Rolls.

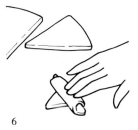

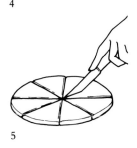

5

6

7

ANADAMA BREAD

½ oz (15 g) fresh yeast or ¼ oz (7 g) dried yeast

4 tablespoons (4 × 15 ml spoon) lukewarm water

3 oz (75 g) cornmeal (polenta)

1½ oz (40 g) butter or margarine

4 tablespoons (4 × 15 ml spoon) black treacle

6 fl oz (175 ml) boiling water

1 egg

1 lb (450 g) strong white flour

2 teaspoons (2 × 5 ml spoon) salt

Oven temperature:
Gas Mark 5/375°F/190°C

There are lots of different tales about this famed bread. One story has it that a fisherman became annoyed with his wife who only gave him cornmeal and molasses for dinner. One day he mixed yeast with flour into the cornmeal and molasses and baked it into a loaf of bread, muttering 'Anna damn her! This is what I like.' Quite right he was, too; it is a beautiful brown bread that rises easily and has a special taste.

Sprinkle the yeast over the lukewarm water and leave it to dissolve. Mix the cornmeal, butter or margarine, treacle and boiling water in a large bowl. When it is lukewarm add the yeast, the egg and half of the flour. Stir together to blend and then add the remaining flour and the salt. Use your hand when it becomes too stiff to stir, and blend until the dough comes away from the sides of the bowl. If it is too sticky add more flour and if too stiff add a little warm water. Knead the dough until it is smooth and elastic. Place the dough in the bowl, cover with a plastic bag and put in a warm place to rise, until the dough doubles in volume (2–3 hours).

Punch down the risen dough with your fist, shape into a rectangle and put in a greased 2 lb (1 kg) loaf tin. It should fill a good half of the tin. Place a plastic bag over the tin and leave to rise again, until the dough is well above the top of the tin (1–2 hours).

Bake the loaf in the centre of the preheated oven for 50 minutes. Turn the loaf out on to a wire rack, or set it across the top of the bread tin, to cool.

BANANA NUT BREAD

8 oz (225 g) plain flour

3 teaspoons (3 × 5 ml spoon) baking powder

1 teaspoon (5 ml spoon) salt

¼ teaspoon (1.25 ml spoon) ground nutmeg

4 oz (100 g) butter

5 oz (150 g) soft light brown sugar

2 eggs

3 well ripened bananas

2 oz (50 g) chopped walnuts

Oven temperature:
Gas Mark 4/350°F/180°C

This is an excellent way of using up very ripe bananas. They give a fragrant taste and a wonderfully moist consistency to this loaf, which slices beautifully and makes an unusual tea bread, either spread with butter or just on its own. The flavour improves when the loaf is kept wrapped in foil.

Grease the bottom of a 2 lb (1 kg) loaf tin and line with greased greaseproof paper. Preheat the oven.

Sift together the flour, baking powder, salt and nutmeg and put aside. Beat the butter and sugar together until light and fluffy. Lightly whisk the eggs and beat into the creamed mixture, a little at a time. Peel the bananas, mash with a fork and add to the mixture. Sift the reserved flour mixture over the creamed mixture a third at a time, stirring until just blended. Lastly, fold in the walnuts.

Pour the mixture into the tin and bake for 1 hour in the preheated oven. Leave in the tin for 10 minutes before turning out on to a rack to cool.

POPOVERS

butter or oil for greasing

2 eggs

8 fl oz (240 ml) milk

½ teaspoon (2.5 ml spoon) salt

3½ oz (75 g) plain flour

1 tablespoon (15 ml spoon) melted butter

Oven temperature:
Gas Mark 7/425°F/220°C

Popovers are also known as Laplanders, Bouncing Babies and Breakfast Puffs. The batter takes only a few minutes to prepare and they come out of the oven all puffed up – crisp and brown on the outside and soft inside. They are as delightful to eat as they are to look at. Serve them hot for breakfast with butter and jam.

Generously grease 12 custard cups set on a baking sheet or a bun tin with wells 1½ inches (4 cm) deep. (The tins must be deep, as the Popovers rise up so much.) Break the eggs into a bowl and add the milk, salt and sifted flour. Whisk together until just blended, disregarding any small lumps. Stir in the melted butter and half-fill the cups with the batter. Place them in a cold oven and set it to the correct temperature. Bake them for 30 minutes (without peeping!) and they should then be puffed up and ready to eat.

Popovers; Philadelphia Sticky Buns; Banana Nut Bread

PHILADELPHIA STICKY BUNS

For the dough:

1 lb (450 g) plain flour

1 teaspoon (5 ml spoon) salt

4 oz (100 g) butter

¼ pint (150 ml) milk

½ oz (15 g) fresh yeast or
¼ oz (7 g) dried yeast

2 tablespoons (2 × 15 ml
spoon) plus 3 oz (75 g)
sugar

2 eggs, beaten lightly

grated rind of 1 lemon

2 teaspoons (2 × 5 ml
spoon) ground cinnamon

4 oz (100 g) raisins or
currants

For the syrup:

8 oz (225 g) soft dark brown
sugar

2 oz (50 g) butter

4 fl oz (110 ml) water

4 oz (100 g) chopped
walnuts

Oven temperature:
Gas Mark 4/350°F/180°C

These are glorified Chelsea buns with a rolled-up filling of raisins and spice. The sticky part is a delectable caramel glaze sprinkled with walnuts that makes the buns extra-special.

To make the dough, sift the flour and salt into a large bowl. Cut the butter into small pieces and rub in. Warm the milk very slightly and add it to the yeast and the 2 tablespoons (2 × 15 ml spoon) sugar. If using dried yeast, set aside for 10 minutes until the yeast is dissolved and the mixture is frothy.

Make a well in the flour and add the yeast mixture, beaten eggs and lemon rind. Stir or mix the dough by hand until it forms a ball and then turn it out on to a floured surface. Knead the dough for 5 minutes, or until it is smooth and elastic. Return it to the bowl and place the bowl in a large plastic bag. Leave in a warm place (70–80°F/21–25°C if possible) until doubled in size, about 2 hours.

Meanwhile, to make the syrup, boil the brown sugar, butter and water together until it becomes a thickish mixture, about 10 minutes. Put 1 tablespoon (15 ml spoon) of the syrup in the bottom of 18 1½-inch (4 cm) deep wells of bun tins or custard cups. If you haven't either of these, use two cake tins and cover the bottoms with the syrup. Sprinkle some of the chopped walnuts into each well or into the tins.

When the dough has doubled in volume, punch it down with your fist and turn it out on to a floured surface. Roll it into a rectangle about 18 × 12 inches (45 × 30 cm). Sprinkle it with the 3 oz (75 g) sugar, the cinnamon and the raisins or currants. Roll the dough into a tight cylinder from the long side and cut it into 1-inch (2.5 cm) rounds. Place each round, cut side up, in a well, or place 9 rounds in each cake tin. Leave in a warm place to rise.

When the dough has risen, bake in the preheated oven for about 25 minutes, placing a sheet of foil under the tins to catch any syrup that bubbles over. Remove the tins from the oven and turn them over on to greaseproof paper. After a few minutes, remove the tins and transfer the buns to a rack to cool.

CORN MUFFINS

Makes approx. 14 muffins or 1 loaf

9 oz (250 g) cornmeal
(polenta)

5 oz (150 g) self-raising
flour

2½ oz (65 g) sugar

1 tablespoon (15 ml spoon)
baking powder

1 teaspoon (5 ml spoon) salt

2 eggs

2 oz (50 g) butter, melted
and cooled

2 oz (50 g) margarine,
melted and cooled

½ pint (300 ml) warm milk

Oven temperature:
Gas Mark 6/400°F/200°C

In America, 'corn' means maize, and what could be more American than Corn Bread, from a country where 'corn grows as high as an elephant's eye'? The Pilgrim Fathers made use of this nourishing grain as the Indians had before them, and it was served in different ways at almost every meal. Crisp-crusted corn muffins, or bread sliced piping hot from the oven, are a great treat with butter and jam. It is perfect for tea or to serve with a meal in place of your usual bread.

Preheat the oven. Sift all the dry ingredients together into a large bowl and put aside. Lightly beat the eggs and then stir in the melted fats and warm milk. Pour into the centre of the dry ingredients and with a large metal spoon fold together until just smooth and blended. Pour into well greased bun tins (about 1½ inches/4 cm deep) or a 9 × 5 × 4-inch (23 × 12 × 10 cm) loaf tin. Bake in the preheated oven, 20 minutes for the muffins or about 35 minutes for the loaf. Serve warm.

BOSTON BROWN BREAD

Makes 2 small loaves

½ pint (300 ml) buttermilk

6 tablespoons (6 × 15 ml spoon) black treacle or molasses

½ oz (15 g) butter, melted

2 oz (50 g) raisins

2½ oz (65 g) rye flour

2½ oz (65 g) 100% wholewheat flour

3 oz (75 g) cornmeal (polenta)

1 teaspoon (5 ml spoon) bicarbonate of soda

1 teaspoon (5 ml spoon) salt

Steamed brown bread served piping hot with Boston Baked Beans was a staple food of Massachusetts and the other colonies, and continues to be enjoyed today. It should be made from two kinds of flour, meal and molasses, which was brought from the West Indies by the New England traders. It is a wonderful and nutritious combination.

Select two empty food cans, approximately 3¼ × 4¼ inches (8 × 11 cm) in size. Wash, dry and grease the bottom and sides thoroughly. Cut out rounds of greaseproof paper and line the bottoms.

In a large bowl, mix the buttermilk, treacle or molasses, butter and raisins together. Combine all the other ingredients and add by quarters to the buttermilk mixture, stirring well after each addition. Fill the cans about two-thirds full and cover with foil lids, tied and taped so that the bread won't force the lids off when it rises. Place the cans in a large saucepan and pour in enough boiling water to come half-way up the sides of the cans. Cover the pan and simmer for 2½ hours.

Turn the bread out on to a warmed dish and serve immediately in slices, with butter for spreading served separately. If you are not using the bread right away it can be kept in its can in the refrigerator for up to a week and steamed for 15 minutes to reheat.

INDIAN PUDDING

Serves 8

1½ pints (900 ml) milk

3 oz (75 g) cornmeal
(polenta)

2 oz (50 g) butter

6 tablespoons (6 × 15 ml
spoon) dark golden syrup
(or half light golden syrup
and half black treacle)

2 eggs

1 teaspoon (5 ml spoon)
ground cinnamon

½ teaspoon (2.5 ml spoon)
ground ginger

2 oz (50 g) raisins
(optional)

To garnish:

grated nutmeg

Oven temperature:
Gas Mark 2/300°F/150°C

Indian pudding is not an original Indian recipe but rather takes its name from its use of cornmeal, which was called Indian meal by the early colonists to avoid confusion with wheat. It is still going strong in New England and if you like milk puddings you should try it. It is particularly good served warm with brandy butter or vanilla ice cream.

Preheat the oven. Heat the milk in a large saucepan until just below a simmer. Slowly add the cornmeal, whisking continuously. Cook together, stirring, over a very low heat until the mixture thickens to a double cream consistency, about 10 minutes. Take off the heat and mix in the other ingredients.

Pour the mixture into a greased baking dish and set the dish in a pan of hot water. Bake in the preheated oven for 1–1½ hours, until the pudding is set. Serve warm with a grating of nutmeg over each serving.

57

VELVET CHEESECAKE

1 oz (25 g) butter

8 digestive biscuits

1 lb (450 g) packaged cream
cheese

3½ oz (90 g) plus
1 tablespoon (15 ml spoon)
caster sugar

4 eggs, separated

grated rind of 1 lemon plus
1 tablespoon (15 ml spoon)
juice

1 tablespoon (15 ml spoon)
plain flour

a small pinch of salt

½ teaspoon (2.5 ml spoon)
vanilla essence (see note
below)

5 fl oz (150 ml) carton of
soured cream

To garnish:

ground cinnamon

Oven temperatures:
Gas Mark 4/350°F/180°C
Gas Mark 5/375°F/190°C

*Early American versions of cheesecake were made
with cottage or curd cheese but today the creamy
version has taken its place and rivals apple pie as a
popular dessert. This is a meltingly good creamy cake
– easy to make and very professional-looking.*

Melt the butter in a small saucepan and set aside.
Crush the biscuits into crumbs. Add the melted
butter and mix together with a fork. Spoon the
mixture into a greased 9-inch (23 cm) cake tin
with a spring–clip side or removable base. Press
the crumbs evenly over the bottom of the tin.

Heat the oven to the first setting. Beat the
cream cheese until it is smooth. Add the 3½ oz
(90 g) of caster sugar and mix until blended. Stir
in the egg yolks, the lemon rind and juice and the
flour. Whisk the egg whites and salt until stiff
but not dry and fold them gently into the cheese
mixture, using a metal spoon. Pour the mixture
into the prepared tin and bake for 35 minutes in
the preheated oven. Remove from the oven and
cool for 15 minutes.

Meanwhile, mix the remaining tablespoon
(15 ml spoon) of caster sugar and the vanilla
essence with the soured cream. Spread evenly
over the top of the cheesecake and dust lightly
with cinnamon.

Turn the oven up to the second setting.
Return the cheesecake to the oven and bake for a
further 10 minutes. Cool and remove the side of
the tin before serving.

Note: vanilla extract is preferable. Ordinary
vanilla flavouring may not give the same results.
Try using vanilla sugar (page 5).

NEW AMSTERDAM APPLE CAKE

Serves 10–12

14 oz (400 g) plain flour

1 teaspoon (5 ml spoon) salt

1 teaspoon (5 ml spoon)
ground cinnamon

1 teaspoon (5 ml spoon)
bicarbonate of soda

2½ lb (1.25 kg) cooking
apples

8 fl oz (240 ml) sunflower
oil

8 oz (225 g) caster sugar

3 eggs

4 oz (100 g) raisins

3 oz (75 g) chopped walnuts

Oven temperature:
Gas Mark 4/350°F/180°C

In New Amsterdam (the old name of New York),
tea-time was a social occasion and an apple cake such
as this one might have been among the assortment of
cakes presented to honoured guests. My guests have
certainly enjoyed it and have often asked for the recipe.
There is a wonderful contrast in the taste and texture
of the brown crunchy top and the soft apple centre. It is
pretty when baked in a tubular shape and the centre
filled with ice cream or whipped cream.

Preheat the oven. Sift together the flour, salt,
cinnamon and soda and set aside. Peel, core and
slice the apples.

Beat the oil and caster sugar together until
well blended. Add the eggs and continue to beat
until the mixture is creamy. Then stir the flour
mixture into this batter. Add the apple slices,
raisins and walnuts (don't be worried if there
seem to be too many apples). Turn the mixture
into a well greased 10-inch (25 cm) cake tin,
tubular for preference. Bake for 1¼ hours in the
preheated oven, or until the sides come away
from the tin. Cool in the tin before turning out.
Serve at room temperature, with ice cream or
whipped cream if desired.

HEALTHY CARROT CAKE

1 tablespoon (15 ml spoon) lemon juice

¼ pint (150 ml) milk

4 oz (100 g) butter

8 fl oz (240 ml) honey

8 oz (225 g) carrots, grated finely

4 oz (100 g) raisins

4 oz (100 g) stoned dates, chopped

1 egg, beaten

4 oz (100 g) 100% wholemeal flour

4 oz (100 g) strong white flour

2 teaspoons (2 × 5 ml spoon) bicarbonate of soda

1 teaspoon (5 ml spoon) baking powder

1 teaspoon (5 ml spoon) ground cinnamon

½ teaspoon (2.5 ml spoon) grated nutmeg

2 oz (50 g) chopped walnuts

Oven temperature:
Gas Mark 4/350°F/180°C

Health foods have taken America by storm and carrot cake is on the menu in health food bakeries and restaurants all over the States. Moist and fragrant, it makes a lovely tea cake that keeps well and is very quick to put together, because no creaming or beating is involved.

Preheat the oven. Grease the bottom of a deep, 8-inch (20 cm) cake tin and line with greased greaseproof paper. Add the lemon juice to the milk and put to one side. Melt the butter and honey in a medium-size saucepan. Then remove from the heat and add the carrots, raisins, dates, egg and reserved soured milk.

Sift the flours with the soda, baking powder, cinnamon and nutmeg. Make a well in the centre of the flour mixture and pour in the carrot mixture. Stir together until blended, add the walnuts and pour into the prepared cake tin. Bake in the centre of the preheated oven for 1–1¼ hours. Leave in the tin to cool partially before turning out on to a rack. Serve warm or cold.

New Amsterdam Apple Cake; Healthy Carrot Cake

APPLE BROWN BETTY

Serves 8

6 oz (175 g) fresh
breadcrumbs

3 oz (75 g) butter

6 oz (175 g) soft light
brown sugar

½ teaspoon (2.5 ml spoon)
ground cinnamon

½ teaspoon (2.5 ml spoon)
grated nutmeg

juice of ½ lemon, plus
1 teaspoon (5 ml spoon)
grated rind

2 lb (900 g) Bramley or
other cooking apples

2 oz (50 g) raisins

Oven temperature:
Gas Mark 5/375°F/190°C

This apple pudding is quickly made and just as quickly eaten! The toasted breadcrumbs and apples combined with spices bake together and make a lovely inexpensive pudding. All New Englanders make a version of this delicious dessert but Betty apparently became famous for hers!

First preheat the oven. Grease a 3–3½-pint (1.7–2-litre) ovenproof dish. Spread the breadcrumbs on a baking sheet and toast under the grill. Cut the butter into small pea-size pieces and put aside. Combine the sugar with the spices and put aside. Put the lemon juice and grated rind in a large bowl. Peel, core and slice the apples and place them immediately in the lemon juice.

Layer the dish with some of the sliced apples, followed by a layer each of raisins, sugar mixture, breadcrumbs and butter. Repeat these layers twice, in the same order. Bake for 30 minutes. Serve warm with cream.

62

PINEAPPLE UPSIDE-DOWN CAKE

4 oz (100 g) butter

6 oz (175 g) soft dark brown sugar

15½ oz (439 g) can of pineapple slices, drained

4 eggs

grated rind of 1 lemon

a pinch of salt

4 oz (100 g) caster sugar

4 oz (100 g) self-raising flour

Oven temperature:
Gas Mark 4/350°F/180°C

White sugar was at one time an expensive luxury and many early American recipes used brown sugar. In this inventive dessert the brown sugar, butter and pineapple rings are put in the bottom of the pan and are later transformed into a scrumptious topping. Traditionally it is made in a skillet (heavy cast-iron frying pan) but if you haven't one that can go in the oven, use a cake tin. Other fruits can be used but pineapple is particularly good.

First preheat the oven. Over a gentle heat melt the butter in an approximately 10-inch (25 cm) ovenproof frying pan. If you haven't one, melt the butter in any pan and then transfer it to a similar-size cake tin. Remove 1 tablespoon (15 ml spoon) of the melted butter and put aside for the cake mixture. Add the brown sugar to the remaining melted butter and stir together until blended. Spread the sugar and butter mixture evenly on the bottom of the pan (or tin) and add the drained pineapple slices in a pretty pattern, covering the surface evenly.

Separate the eggs, dropping the yolks into a small bowl and the whites into a larger one. Beat the yolks with the reserved tablespoon (15 ml spoon) of melted butter and the grated lemon rind. Whisk the egg whites with the salt until stiff. Fold in the sugar, little by little, and then the yolk mixture. Sift the flour and carefully fold it in, a third at a time, using a metal spoon. Pour over the pineapple and bake for 30 minutes.

Remove the cake from the oven (don't forget an oven glove for the handle of the frying pan, if used). While still hot, place a serving plate on top of the pan, bottom-side up, and with a quick movement turn upside-down. Serve hot or cold, with whipped cream or on its own.

STRAWBERRY SHORTCAKE

Serves 8

7 oz (200 g) strong white flour

2 tablespoons (2 × 15 ml spoon) caster sugar

¼ teaspoon (1.25 ml spoon) salt

3 teaspoons (3 × 5 ml spoon) baking powder

2½ oz (65 g) butter, plus a knob for buttering

¼ pint (150 ml) milk

2 lb (900 g) fresh strawberries

2–3 oz (50–75 g) sugar

juice of ½ lemon

½ pint (300 ml) double or whipping cream

Oven temperature:
Gas Mark 7/425°F/220°C

In 1643 Roger Williams, the founder of Providence, Rhode Island, wrote in his Key into the Language of the Indians of America that the strawberry 'is the wonder of all the Fruits growing naturally in those parts. In some parts where the Natives have planted, I have many times seen as many as would fill a good ship, within a few miles compasse.' Recipes for Strawberry Shortcake date back to this time. The crisp shortcake is split into two and buttered while still warm before being filled with strawberries and cream It is delicious and makes a very attractive dessert.

Preheat the oven. Sift the flour, caster sugar, salt and baking powder together. Cut the 2½ oz (65 g) butter into the dry ingredients and rub with your fingertips until the mixture is crumb-like. Pour in the milk and stir with a spoon until a soft dough is formed. Roll the dough out on a floured surface until ¼ inch (5 mm) thick. Cut into 8 rounds, 3 inches (8 cm) in diameter, and place the rounds on a lightly greased baking sheet. Bake in the preheated oven for 12 minutes or until golden brown.

Meanwhile, slice two-thirds of the strawberries and mix them with the sugar and the lemon juice. Refrigerate until needed. Whip the cream and set aside.

Split the shortcakes in two and while still warm butter one half of each inside. Place each buttered half facing up on an individual serving dish and cover with sliced strawberries and a dollop of cream. Cover this with the other half of the shortcake and place some whole strawberries on top with more cream. (If you have baked the shortcakes in advance, warm them in the oven to crisp them before buttering and serving warm with the strawberries and cream.)

Strawberry Shortcake

PUMPKIN PIE

For the pastry:

6 oz (175 g) flour

½ teaspoon (2.5 ml spoon) salt

1 tablespoon (15 ml spoon) sugar

1 teaspoon (5 ml spoon) baking powder

3 oz (75 g) unsalted butter, very cold

1 egg yolk

3–4 tablespoons (3–4 × 15 ml spoon) double cream

For the filling:

1 lb (450 g) pumpkin pulp (using about 2 lb/900 g pumpkin – see Pumpkin Soup recipe, page 8)

2 large (size 1–2) or 3 small (size 4–5) eggs

3 oz (75 g) soft brown sugar

4 tablespoons (4 × 15 ml spoon) golden syrup

8 fl oz (240 ml) whipping or double cream

1½ teaspoons (3 × 2.5 ml spoon) ground cinnamon

1 teaspoon (5 ml spoon) ground ginger

¼ teaspoon (1.25 ml spoon) ground cloves

½ teaspoon (2.5 ml spoon) salt

Oven temperatures:
Gas Mark 6/400°F/200°C
Gas Mark 5/375°F/190°C

A Thanksgiving 'must', Pumpkin Pie is related to the English custard pie. The pumpkin gives the pie great lightness and the brown sugar provides the flavour. Jack o' lanterns with cut-out eyes and toothy grins made from pumpkins are seen everywhere on Hallowe'en. Children enjoy cutting out the faces and the firm flesh can serve as a purée for the pie.

To make the pastry, sift the flour, salt, sugar and baking powder into a mixing bowl. Cut the butter into small pieces and rub into the mixture with the tips of your fingers until the mixture acquires the texture of oatmeal. Blend the egg yolk and cream together and, using a fork, stir into the flour mixture. Turn the dough out on to a lightly floured surface and knead for 10 seconds with the heel of your hand to blend. Wrap the dough in cling film and refrigerate for at least 30 minutes.

Roll out the dough when ready and line a 9½–10-inch (24–25 cm) pie plate. Prick the base with a fork and fill the centre with a piece of crumpled greaseproof paper weighed down with dried beans or rice. Refrigerate for 15 minutes before baking blind at the first setting for 15 minutes. Remove the paper and beans for the last 5 minutes of the cooking time. Place on a rack to cool.

Combine all the filling ingredients and mix together until just blended. Pour into the pie case and return to the oven at the lower setting for 40 minutes, or until the filling has set. If you place the pie plate on a hot baking sheet in the oven while it cooks it helps keep the bottom pastry crisp. Serve at room temperature, with cream if desired.

PECAN PIE

Serves 8

Basic pastry recipe: see Pumpkin Pie, opposite

For the pastry:

ingredients as Pumpkin Pie
pastry

For the filling:

3 eggs

8 oz (225 g) soft dark brown
sugar

1 teaspoon (5 ml spoon)
vanilla essence (see note
below)

¼ teaspoon (1.25 ml
spoon) salt

3 oz (75 g) butter, melted

6 tablespoons (6 × 15 ml
spoon) dark golden syrup
(or half light golden syrup
and half black treacle)

8 oz (225 g) shelled pecan
nuts, chopped coarsely, plus
a few halved to decorate

Oven temperatures:
Gas Mark 6/400°F/200°C
Gas Mark 4/350°F/180°C

*Pecan nuts are grown in the southern states and are the
inspiration for this most delicious pie. It is a first
cousin to the treacle tart but the pecans make it unique.
In 'bake-offs' it always wins a prize. It is at its most
delectable served warm with vanilla ice cream.*

Make the pastry and form a pie shell as for
Pumpkin Pie, and bake blind at the first oven
setting. Turn the oven down to the second
setting. Lightly beat the eggs in a medium-size
bowl. Beat in the sugar, vanilla essence and salt.
Stir in the melted butter, syrup and chopped
nuts. Pour into the partially baked pie shell and
decorate with the pecan halves.

Bake in the middle of the oven on a hot baking
sheet for 35– 40 minutes or until the filling is set.
Cover with foil if the pastry becomes too dark.
Serve warm or cool with ice cream or cream.

Note: vanilla extract is preferable. Ordinary
vanilla flavouring may not give the same results.
Try using vanilla sugar (page 5).

BLUEBERRY PIE

Basic pastry recipe: see Pumpkin Pie, page 66

For the pastry:

double the ingredients for
Pumpkin Pie pastry

For the filling:

1 lb (450 g) blueberries,
fresh or frozen

3 oz (75 g) sugar

2 tablespoons (2 × 15 ml
spoon) plain flour

2 tablespoons (2 × 15 ml
spoon) lemon juice

½ oz (15 g) butter

Oven temperatures:
Gas Mark 6/400°F/200°C
Gas Mark 4/350°F/180°C

Blueberries grow in abundance in the United States, and now, happily, are cultivated here in the West Country. They are available in July and August and are a real treat to look forward to. In this pie the combination of the rich purple filling contained between two layers of golden pastry is irresistibly good. Serve warm or cold and, for an extra-special treat, with vanilla ice cream.

Make the pastry and chill for 30 minutes or longer. Then divide it in two and roll out and line a 9–inch (23 cm) dish with one half.

Mix the blueberries, sugar, flour and lemon juice together. Spoon into the pie shell and dot with the butter. Roll out the remaining pastry and cover, joining the edges carefully. Slash the top in several places to allow steam to escape.

Bake in the oven preheated to the first setting for 10 minutes and then reduce the heat to the second setting and bake 20 minutes longer, or until the pastry is golden brown. If you place the pie dish on a hot baking sheet the bottom pastry will be crisper. Serve either warm or cold.

Pecan Pie; Blueberry Pie; Key Lime Pie

KEY LIME PIE

2 oz (50 g) butter

8 digestive biscuits

3 egg yolks

14 oz (397 g) can of
sweetened condensed milk

4 fl oz (110 ml) fresh lime
juice (about 3 limes), plus
grated rind of 1 lime

a few drops of green food
colouring

5 fl oz (150 ml) carton of
double or whipping cream
(optional)

*This pie originated in Key West, Florida, where the
limes are smaller and juicier than normal. It is
delicious made with any limes, however, and
incredibly easy and quick to prepare, requiring no
cooking. When refrigerated the pie sets into a silky
custard with a fresh tart flavour. It can be decorated
with whipped cream to make it even more delectable.*

Melt the butter in a small saucepan and set aside.
Crush the biscuits into fine crumbs, add the
melted butter and mix together with a fork.
Spoon the mixture into a greased 8–9-inch (20–
23 cm) dish and press the crumbs evenly over the
bottom. Refrigerate until ready to fill.
  In a medium-size bowl, beat the egg yolks
with a whisk or rotary beater (electric or hand)
for 5 minutes until they are thick. Beat in the
condensed milk, lime juice, grated rind and
colouring. Pour the mixture into the pie shell
and refrigerate for at least 4 hours, or until it is
set. Before serving, whip the cream and pipe or
spoon decorative swirls over the top.

EASY GRAPE PUDDING

9 oz (250 g) thick-set
natural yogurt or soured
cream

1 lb (450 g) seedless white
grapes

2–2½ oz (50–65 g) soft
brown sugar

*This superb quick pudding is popular in America and
comes as a happy surprise when I serve it here.
Seedless grapes, yogurt and brown sugar are the magic
ingredients and quite delicious when served chilled.
Do try it.*

When buying white grapes, pick the bunches
with golden rather than green grapes. Wash and
dry the grapes and pull off all the stems. Mix
them with the yogurt or soured cream. Place the
mixture in a shallow dish and press level.
Sprinkle the brown sugar over the top and
refrigerate. This dish can be made several hours
ahead of time.

TOLL HOUSE COOKIES

4 oz (100 g) butter

1½ oz (40 g) granulated sugar

3 oz (75 g) soft dark brown sugar

1 egg

½ teaspoon (2.5 ml spoon) vanilla essence (see note below)

4 oz (100 g) plain flour

½ teaspoon (2.5 ml spoon) bicarbonate of soda

½ teaspoon (2.5 ml spoon) salt

4 oz (100 g) bar of plain chocolate, cut into pea-size pieces

2 oz (50 g) chopped walnuts

Oven temperature:
Gas Mark 4/350°F/180°C

In the days when you had to pay for crossing the Mississippi River it was possible to rest and buy coffee and cookies in the house of the toll-man. Toll House Cookies, often known as chocolate chip cookies, are world-famous. When you smell them baking and taste them you will understand their lasting popularity.

First preheat the oven. Cream the butter and the two sugars together until light and fluffy. Lightly mix the egg and vanilla essence and gradually beat into the creamed mixture. Sift together the flour, bicarbonate of soda and salt and stir into the mixture. Finally stir in the chocolate bits and the walnuts.

Spoon heaped teaspoons of the mixture on to greased baking sheets, well spaced out, as they spread a lot. Bake for 10–15 minutes, or until light brown. Remove the cookies with a spatula while they are hot and place on any flat surface to cool. They will become crisp as they cool. Store in an airtight tin.

Note: vanilla extract is preferable. Ordinary vanilla flavouring may not give the same results. Try using vanilla sugar (page 5).

CHOCOLATE DEVIL'S FOOD CAKE

For the cake:

1 tablespoon (15 ml spoon) lemon juice or vinegar

8 fl oz (240 ml) milk

8 oz (225 g) plain flour

1 teaspoon (5 ml spoon) bicarbonate of soda

2 oz (50 g) cocoa powder

4 oz (100 g) butter or margarine, softened

9 oz (250 g) caster sugar

2 large eggs (size 1–2)

For the soured cream frosting:

9 oz (250 g) plain chocolate, broken into small pieces

a pinch of salt

3 tablespoons (3 × 15 ml spoon) caster sugar

½ pint (300 ml) soured cream

For filling (optional):

whipped cream

Oven temperature:
Gas Mark 4/350°F/180°C

No one seems to know how this cake came by its name. Perhaps with the invention of Angel Food Cake there had to be a Devil's Food Cake. Whatever its origins, it well deserves its fame. It is a scrumptious cake – chocolaty, moist and light and amazingly easy to make successfully. I love it with chocolate soured cream frosting, which is also quickly made: if you have more time, try fudge icing (see variation of Chocolate Fudge, page 90).

To make the cake, add the lemon juice or vinegar to the milk and put aside. Grease and line two 8–9-inch (20–23 cm) sandwich tins with greased greaseproof paper discs. Sift the flour, bicarbonate of soda and cocoa together. Preheat the oven.

In a large bowl, cream the butter or margarine with half the sugar until light. Gradually beat in the eggs and then mix in the rest of the sugar. Add the reserved soured milk alternately with the cocoa mixture. Divide the resulting mixture between the two tins and spread level. Bake in the centre of the oven for 30 minutes. Leave in the tins for 10 minutes before turning out on to a wire rack to cool.

To make the frosting, simply melt the chocolate in the top of a double boiler or in a bowl over a pan of boiling water and then whisk in the salt, sugar and soured cream.

You can slice the layers of cake in half to make four discs and then sandwich with the frosting before icing the top. If you prefer a lighter cake, however, you could make only half the amount of frosting and alternate the layers with whipped cream, again icing the top.

Chocolate Devil's Food Cake

ANGEL FOOD CAKE

5 egg whites

1¾ oz (45 g) fine plain flour, sifted with
1 tablespoon (15 ml spoon) cornflour

5 oz (150 g) caster sugar

1 tablespoon (15 ml spoon) water

a pinch of salt

½ teaspoon (2.5 ml spoon) cream of tartar

½ teaspoon (2.5 ml spoon) vanilla essence (see note below)

Oven temperatures:
Gas Mark 5/375°F/190°C
Gas Mark 1/275°F/140°C

This soufflé-light cake is popular all over the States. Although it is usually baked in a tubular tin you can bake it in any shape, as long as the pan is absolutely free of grease, for the cake must cling to the sides as it rises. It is very versatile – wonderful with ice cream or fruit or with a chocolate sauce. It is also delicious with a thin orange or lemon butter icing. It does not freeze well, because it has no fat content.

Allow the egg whites to warm to room temperature if necessary. Preheat the oven to the first setting. Sift the flour with 2 oz (50 g) of the caster sugar three times and set aside.

Whisk the egg whites with the water and salt until just foamy. Sift in the cream of tartar and continue to whisk until the mixture will stand in peaks. Whisk in the remaining caster sugar, 2 tablespoons (2 × 15 ml spoon) at a time, and the vanilla essence. The mixture should be thick and quite stiff but not dry. Sift about a quarter of the flour and sugar mixture over the egg whites and gently fold it in with a metal spoon. Continue, a quarter at a time, until all the flour is used.

Pour the batter into an ungreased 8–9-inch (20–23 cm) tin (tubular if possible) and bake in the centre of the oven for 15 minutes. Lower the oven to the second setting and continue to bake for another 15 minutes. Turn upside-down on a wire rack until cool before removing from the tin. To serve, cut with a serrated knife.

Note: vanilla extract is preferable. Ordinary vanilla flavouring may not give the same results. Try using vanilla sugar (page 5).

HERMITS

4 oz (100 g) plain flour

1½ teaspoons (3 × 2.5 ml spoon) baking powder

1 teaspoon (5 ml spoon) ground cinnamon

¼ teaspoon (1.25 ml spoon) ground nutmeg

¼ teaspoon (1.25 ml spoon) ground mace

¼ teaspoon (1.25 ml spoon) ground cloves

¼ teaspoon (1.25 ml spoon) ground allspice

8 oz (225 g) raisins

4½ oz (115 g) butter

3 oz (75 g) caster sugar

2 eggs

4 fl oz (110 ml) black treacle or molasses

2 oz (50 g) chopped walnuts

For decoration (optional):

2 oz (50 g) icing sugar

1½ teaspoons (3 × 2.5 ml spoon) lemon juice

Oven temperature:
Gas Mark 4/350°F/180°C

New England cooks loved giving their cakes and biscuits amusing names. Perhaps the dark colour of these spicy bars reminded them of a hermit's cave! They are perfect to include in lunch boxes and picnic baskets.

Preheat the oven. Line the bottom of a 13 × 9-inch (33 × 23 cm) swiss roll tin with greased greaseproof paper. Sift together the flour, baking powder and spices. Place the raisins in a bowl and toss with a few tablespoons of the flour mixture.

In another, large, bowl, cream the butter and caster sugar until light and fluffy. Beat in the eggs, little by little, and then the treacle or molasses. Stir in the flour mixture and then the raisins and walnuts. Spread in the prepared tin and bake in the centre of the oven for 15–20 minutes. Leave in the pan to cool and then cut into bars before serving.

For a more decorative finish, sift the icing sugar and stir into the lemon juice. Using a teaspoon, dribble the mixture over the Hermits.

BROWNIES

4 oz (100 g) butter

1–1½ oz (25–40 g) cocoa powder

2 eggs

8 oz (225 g) caster sugar

1 teaspoon (5 ml spoon) vanilla essence (see note below)

2 oz (50 g) self-raising flour

2–4 oz (50–100 g) chopped walnuts

2 oz (50 g) raisins (optional)

Oven temperature:
Gas Mark 4/350°F/180°C

If you have never tasted an American Brownie you are in for a treat. These delectable chocolate squares are made at home and in bakeries across America. It is customary to use baker's unsweetened chocolate but as this is hard to come by here I use cocoa, with very good results. One important point is not to overcook them. They should be moist inside and chewy. When they cool they firm up a bit. They are good on any occasion and children, as well as even the most gourmet-minded grown-ups, are delighted with them.

Grease an 8-inch (20 cm) square, shallow cake tin and line the bottom with greased greaseproof paper. Preheat the oven. Gently melt the butter in a small saucepan, stir in the cocoa until blended and set aside.

In a medium-size bowl, beat the eggs and caster sugar together until light and add the cocoa mixture. Stir in the vanilla essence and then sift over the flour and mix in. Add the nuts, and raisins if used, and turn into the prepared tin.

Bake in the centre of the oven for 30–35 minutes. Allow to cool for 10 minutes in the tin before cutting into 2-inch (5 cm) squares and removing to a rack to finish cooling.

Note: vanilla extract is preferable. Ordinary vanilla flavouring may not give the same results. Try using vanilla sugar (page 5).

Peanut Butter Cookies; Brownies; Hermits; Angel Food Cake

PEANUT BUTTER COOKIES

5 oz (150 g) plain flour

½ teaspoon (2.5 ml spoon) bicarbonate of soda

½ teaspoon (2.5 ml spoon) salt

4 oz (100 g) butter

3 oz (75 g) soft dark brown sugar

3 oz (75 g) granulated sugar

1 egg

½ teaspoon (2.5 ml spoon) vanilla essence (see note below)

8 oz (225 g) crunchy peanut butter

Oven temperature:
Gas Mark 4/350°F/180°C

In the eighteenth century peanut crops were recorded by Thomas Jefferson in his plantation ledger, but it was not until the next century that peanut cultivation was widespread and it became such a popular food. Even if you are not a fan of peanut butter these cookies will convert you. They are crunchy and crumbly and have a wonderful flavour. A great favourite in my household.

Sift together the flour, bicarbonate of soda and salt and set aside. Cream the butter and both sugars until soft and fluffy. Lightly mix the egg and vanilla essence together and gradually beat into the creamed mixture. Stir in the peanut butter and blend well. Finally stir in the sifted flour. (If you have the time to refrigerate the dough for 1 hour or longer it will make it firmer and easier to handle.)

Spoon out rounded teaspoons of the mixture and roll into balls. Place on greased baking sheets and press flat with a fork into rounds approximately 1½ inches (4 cm) across.

Bake in the preheated oven for 15 minutes. Lift the cookies from the baking sheet with a spatula and cool before serving.

Note: vanilla extract is preferable. Ordinary vanilla flavouring may not give the same results. Try using vanilla sugar (page 5).

OATMEAL LACE COOKIES

Makes 36

5 oz (150 g) oat flakes

4 oz (100 g) soft dark brown
sugar

4 oz (100 g) granulated
sugar

3 tablespoons (3 × 15 ml
spoon) plain flour

5 oz (150 g) butter

1 egg, beaten lightly

1 teaspoon (5 ml spoon)
vanilla extract (see note)

2½ oz (65 g) chopped
hazelnuts

salt (optional)

Oven temperature:
Gas Mark 5/375°F/190°C

*Americans make very good cookies and these are no
exception. They are quick to make and have a thin
lacy elegance. Perfect with fruit or ice cream.*

Preheat the oven. Mix the oats, brown and
white sugar and flour in a bowl. Melt the butter
and pour it into the centre of the dry ingredients.
Stir in the beaten egg and vanilla and then fold in
the nuts. If you have used unsalted butter, add a
good pinch of salt.

Drop tablespoons (15 ml spoon) of the batter
on to ungreased baking sheets, leaving space
between them for spreading. Bake for 5–8
minutes until the edges are lightly browned and
they are bubbling all over. Let them cool on the
sheets before removing with a spatula to a cake
rack. Store in an airtight container when cold.

Note: try using vanilla sugar instead of the
granulated sugar (see page 5).

PECAN POUND CAKE

Makes a 9-inch (23 cm) cake

9 oz (250 g) self-raising
flour

9 oz (250 g) butter, softened

9 oz (250 g) caster sugar

4 eggs, separated

8 tablespoons (8 × 15 ml
spoon) brandy

a pinch of salt

4 oz (100 g) pecan nuts,
chopped

Oven temperature:
Gas Mark 4/350°F/180°C

*Pound cakes enjoy a wide popularity all across the
States. This is a Southern version that travels superbly.*

Preheat the oven. Grease a 9-inch (23 cm) round
deep cake tin and line with greaseproof paper.
Sift the flour on to a plate. Cream the butter with
three-quarters of the sugar until light and fluffy
and add the egg yolks, one at a time, beating well
after each addition. Add the brandy.

Whisk the egg whites with the pinch of salt
until stiff, then whisk in the remaining sugar.
Fold the egg whites and flour alternately into the
creamed mixture. Fold in the chopped nuts and
spoon into the prepared tin.

Bake the cake for about 50 minutes. Allow the
cake to cool in the tin before turning out. Cool
complete before storing in an airtight container.

79

CRANBERRY PIE

Serves 8

Basic pastry recipe: see Pumpkin Pie, page 66

For the pastry:

1½ times the ingredients for Pumpkin Pie pastry

For the filling:

12 oz (350 g) cranberries, fresh or frozen

8 oz (225 g) sugar

a pinch of salt

1 tablespoon (15 ml spoon) grated orange rind

¼ pint (150 ml) fresh orange juice

3 tablespoons (3 × 15 ml spoon) plain flour

2 oz (50 g) chopped walnuts

3 oz (75 g) raisins

1½ oz (40 g) butter

Oven temperature:
Gas Mark 6/400°F/200°C

The bright red cranberry has its place as part of the Thanksgiving tradition in the form of cranberry sauce or relish, but with its special tartness and flavour it has many more uses. Try putting some in the next apple pie you bake, for instance. One of my favourite ways of enjoying them is in this Cranberry Pie. The raisins and walnuts add a delicious contrast of tastes and the rich red colour of the cranberries under the lattice pastry top looks beautiful.

Make the pastry and chill for 30 minutes. Meanwhile, pick over the cranberries, discarding any that are soft and withered. Coarsely chop them, either with a knife or by putting them in a processor and turning it on and off every few seconds. Combine all the rest of the ingredients, except the butter, in a bowl and mix in the cranberries.

Preheat the oven. Line a 9-inch (23 cm) pie dish with two-thirds of the pastry. Roll out the remaining pastry and cut it into lattice strips ½ inch (1 cm) wide. Pour the cranberry mixture into the pie shell and dot with the butter. Cover with the strips to make a lattice top. Bake the pie for 30 minutes. If you place the pie tin on a hot baking sheet in the oven it will make the bottom pastry nice and crisp. Serve warm.

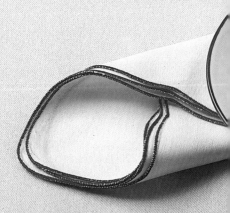

Cranberry Pie

Pancakes with maple syrup

81

PANCAKES

8 oz (225 g) plain flour

3 teaspoons (3 × 5 ml spoon) baking powder

1 teaspoon (5 ml spoon) sugar

a good pinch of salt

2 small eggs

8 fl oz (240 ml) milk

1 oz (25 g) butter, plus a little extra for spreading

maple syrup or thin honey

The American pancake is altogether heartier and more filling than the European crêpe. Popular for breakfast, a pile of pancakes (or a 'stack of wheat') was a good start to a hard day's work in the fields for the early settlers of pioneer America. The batter is dropped by spoonfuls on to a sizzling hot griddle and the result is airy and thick instead of paper-thin. What could be better than a steaming pile laced with butter and topped with maple syrup!

Sift the dry ingredients into a bowl. Make a well in the centre, break in the eggs and add the milk. Stir with a wooden spoon from the centre, slowly incorporating the flour from the sides as you stir. Don't over-mix or worry about small lumps.

Melt the butter in a heavy frying pan and then tip it into the batter. Put the frying pan back over the heat and when it is nice and hot pour large spoonfuls of the batter into the pan to form 3-inch (7.5 cm) pancakes. They should make a sizzling sound and begin to bubble at once. When they look dry at the edges, turn them. They should have a good brown colour. The second side will cook more quickly than the first. Place them on a platter, cover with a tea-towel and keep warm in a low oven while you make the rest. Serve with a little extra softened butter and maple syrup or honey.

CONSERVES AND RELISHES

APPLE BUTTER

Makes approx. 5 lb (2.25 kg)

4 lb (1.8 kg) cooking apples

¾ pint (450 ml) dry cider

approx. 1 lb (450 g) soft light brown sugar

1 teaspoon (5 ml spoon) ground cinnamon

½ teaspoon (2.5 ml spoon) ground cloves

½ teaspoon (2.5 ml spoon) ground allspice

When sugar was scarce in early American kitchens fruit 'butters' were frequently made – long, slow boiling concentrated the flavour and the natural sugar of the fruit provided a sweet, jam-like spread. Today Apple Butter, with its spicy apple taste, is still loved and made in many homes.

Wash and quarter (but do not peel) the apples and place with the cider in a large saucepan. Cook, covered, until the apples are soft and then purée them through a mouli or a sieve. Measure the purée and allow 1 oz (25 g) of sugar for every 4 fl oz (110 ml) of purée.

Return the purée to the saucepan with the measured amount of sugar and the spices and boil slowly, stirring, until very thick (about 1 hour). When a small amount on a saucer holds its shape if turned upside-down it is cooked. Alternatively, you can thicken the purée by cooking uncovered in a slow oven with just an occasional stir. Spoon, while still hot, into sterilised jars and seal.

PICKLED PRUNES

Makes approx. 4 lb (1.8 kg)

2 lb (900 g) dried prunes
water or weak tea
1 lb (450 g) sugar
¾ pint (450 ml) cider vinegar
4 cloves
3 tablespoons (3 × 15 ml spoon) allspice berries
1 stick of cinnamon
a small piece of root ginger, peeled (optional)
rind of 1 lemon, cut into narrow strips

I find these lovely, mildly spiced prunes wonderful for all kinds of dishes – to accompany cold and hot meats, particularly pork, and in stuffings for, say, a boned lamb shoulder. Their round, dark, shiny shapes look attractive and they taste delectable.

Soak the prunes overnight in just enough water or weak tea to cover.

In a large saucepan, dissolve the sugar in the vinegar and then add the spices and lemon rind. Next add the prunes with their liquid and boil very gently for 15 minutes. Remove the prunes and pack into hot, sterilised jars. Boil down the syrup until thick, about 15 minutes, and pour over the prunes to fill the jars before sealing.

These pickles improve with keeping and should be left for at least 4 weeks before using.

BREAD AND BUTTER PICKLES

Makes approx. 4 lb (1.8 kg)

2 lb (900 g) cucumbers (about 2 large ones), cut into ¼-inch (5 mm) slices
12 oz (350 g) onions, sliced very thinly
2 oz (50 g) salt
12 fl oz (350 ml) cider vinegar
12 oz (350 g) sugar
2 tablespoons (2 × 15 ml spoon) mustard seed
2 teaspoons (2 × 5 ml spoon) celery seed
¼ teaspoon (1.25 ml spoon) turmeric
¼ teaspoon (1.25 ml spoon) cayenne pepper

This sweet–sour cucumber pickle is good enough to eat on its own with bread and butter. It is just the thing to have handy to add last-minute zest to a meal.

Put the sliced cucumbers with the onions and salt in a large bowl. Mix together well and allow to stand for 3 hours. Drain and rinse well under cold water and drain again.

Bring all the other ingredients to the boil in a large pan and then add the cucumbers and onions. Reduce the heat and bring just to a simmer, cooking for 2 minutes. Do not allow it to boil or the finished pickles will be too limp. Pour the cucumbers into hot, sterilised jars and cover with the liquid, spices and onions before sealing.

Baked Glazed Gammon (recipe on page 33); Cranberry–Orange Relish; Pickled Prunes; Bread and Butter Pickles

CRANBERRY–ORANGE RELISH

Makes 2 lb (900 g)

4 fl oz (110 ml) orange juice

4 fl oz (110 ml) water

8 oz (225 g) sugar

1 lb (450 g) whole cranberries, fresh or frozen

2 tablespoons (2 × 15 ml spoon) grated orange rind

'Bogland medicine' made from the cranberry, rich in vitamin C, was carried in barrels on the early colonists' ships to prevent scurvy. They were also known at this time as bounceberries, since they were, and still are, tested for their ripeness by their ability to bounce. Cranberry–Orange Relish is a beautiful red colour and its tart flavour is a delicious accompaniment to poultry or pork.

Mix the orange juice, water and sugar in a saucepan and heat together until the sugar is dissolved (7–8 minutes). Add the cranberries, bring to the boil and cook for 3–5 minutes, or until the skins of the berries begin to pop. Remove from the heat and stir in the orange rind. Pour into hot, sterilised jars and seal, or if you are using it soon allow it to cool and chill it before serving.

SNACKS AND CANDIES

QUICK DIPS

Many Americans have only a sandwich lunch and by drinks time before the evening meal they are hungry and ready for an appetiser. Dips are very popular. They can be made quickly and are delicious and attractive when surrounded by a wide variety of raw vegetables, crisps or crackers.

6 oz (175 g) can of crabmeat

8 oz (225 g) cream cheese

1 tablespoon (15 ml spoon) lemon juice

salt and freshly ground black pepper

Oven temperature:
Gas Mark 4/350°F/180°C

Hot Crab Dip

Drain the crabmeat and mix with the cream cheese and lemon juice. Season well with salt and pepper. Bake, uncovered, in the preheated oven for 15 minutes. Can also be served spread on crackers. Serve hot.

2 × 14 oz (397 g) can of artichoke hearts

8 fl oz (225 ml) mayonnaise, home-made or a good commercial kind

3 oz (75 g) grated parmesan cheese

Oven temperature:
Gas Mark 4/350°F/180°C

Artichoke Dip

Drain the artichokes and rinse in cold running water. Drain again, squeezing out as much moisture as possible. Mix with the other ingredients, roughly mashing the artichokes. Bake, uncovered, in preheated oven at until the mixture is bubbling (about 20 minutes). Can also be served spread on crackers. Serve hot.

Soured Cream Dips

Soured Cream Curry Dip: fry a very finely chopped small onion in 1 oz (25 g) butter until soft. Add 1 tablespoon (15 ml spoon) curry powder and cook together for a few minutes. Pour into a bowl and mix in ½ pint (300 ml) soured cream and 3 tablespoons (3 × 15 ml spoon) mayonnaise. Add salt and pepper to taste. You can also add some chutney if you wish.

Soured Cream Herb Dip: add 2 oz (50 g) mixed, finely chopped parsley and chives (or other fresh herbs) to ½ pint (300 ml) soured cream and 3 tablespoons (3 × 15 ml spoon) mayonnaise. Add salt and pepper to taste.

Soured Cream Cheese Dip: add whatever strong cheese you have on hand, crumbled or grated, to soured cream. Stilton, blue cheese or mature Cheddar are good. Use about 5 oz (150 g) cheese to ½ pint (300 ml) soured cream, depending on the strength of the cheese. You can also add 2 teaspoons (2 × 5 ml spoon) Dijon-type mustard or chopped chives.

CRUNCHY MUESLI

3 cups oat flakes plus 3 cups of other cereal flakes, such as wheat, barley or rye or 6 cups of a muesli base which uses cereal flakes

1 cup desiccated coconut

1 cup sunflower seeds

½ cup sesame seeds

½ cup sunflower oil

½ cup honey

1 teaspoon (5 ml spoon) vanilla essence (see note below)

½ – 1 cup raisins or other dried fruit

Oven temperature:
Gas Mark ½ / 250°F / 130°C

Although Muesli originated in Switzerland, America invented the crunchy sort. You can make the most delicious kind at home and vary the ingredients each time you make a new batch – there is such a wide variety of dried fruit and nuts available now. My children eat it like a sweet, by the handful, and I find it hard to pass the large glass jar that I store it in without a nibble. Serve it with milk as you would any breakfast cereal. It is easier to use a cup for the measurements – any average teacup will do.

Preheat the oven. Mix the cereal flakes, coconut, sunflower seeds and sesame seeds together and spread out on a large baking sheet.

Gently heat the oil and honey together, stirring until blended. Take off the heat and mix in the vanilla essence. Pour over the muesli and bake for 1 hour, stirring and turning over with a spatula from time to time to toast evenly. Remove from the oven and add the dried fruit. When it is cool, store in a jar with a tight-fitting lid.

Note: vanilla extract is preferable. Ordinary vanilla flavouring may not give the same results. Try using vanilla sugar (page 5).

Crunchy Muesli

CHOCOLATE FUDGE

8 fl oz (240 ml) milk

2 tablespoons (2 × 15 ml spoon) golden syrup

14 oz (400 g) granulated sugar

4 oz (100 g) unsalted butter

a pinch of salt

1½ oz (40 g) cocoa powder

1 teaspoon (5 ml spoon) vanilla essence (see note below)

2 oz (50 g) chopped walnuts

This makes the most wonderfully creamy, chocolate fudge imaginable. English fudge is often granular in its consistency but this is a rich, smooth, American-style fudge. The trick is to cool it slightly before beating in the cocoa and quickly pour it into a tin before it sets. It cannot help but be your favourite once you have tasted it.

Combine the milk, syrup and sugar in a fairly large, heavy-based saucepan and stir over a low heat until the sugar is dissolved. Make sure the sugar dissolves before the syrup boils. Continue to cook over a slightly higher temperature without stirring (unless it threatens to stick) until the temperature reaches 234°F/112°C on a sugar thermometer, or until a little syrup dropped into a saucer of cold water will hold its shape if it is rolled into a soft ball between finger and thumb – about 30 minutes. (It is often tricky to know exactly how soft the ball should be and I find that, when I place a ball on a smooth surface, if it holds its shape but slowly spreads it is ready.)

When the syrup is ready, take the pan off the heat and add half the butter, cut into a few pieces. Do not stir it in but allow it to melt on the surface of the syrup.

Meanwhile, gently melt the remaining 2 oz (50 g) butter. Remove the melted butter from the heat and stir in a pinch of salt, the cocoa and the vanilla essence. When your hands can just be held against the sides of the saucepan with the syrup in it, quickly stir in the cocoa mixture and the walnuts and beat with a wooden spoon until it is creamy. Immediately pour it into a buttered, shallow 7-inch (18 cm) square pan. Mark into squares while still warm, then leave until it is set before cutting and serving. Store any that is left in a tightly closed tin.

Variation: the same recipe can be used for fudge icing. Add 1–2 tablespoons (1–2 × 15 ml spoon) of boiling water with the cocoa mixture to the sugar syrup before beating and spreading on a cake (such as Chocolate Devil's Food Cake, page 72).

Note: vanilla extract is preferable. Ordinary vanilla flavouring may not give the same results. Try using vanilla sugar (page 5).

PEANUT BRITTLE

Makes 1¾ lb (775 g)

12 oz (350 g) granulated sugar

6 fl oz (175 ml) golden syrup

6 fl oz (175 ml) water

10 oz (275 g) salted roasted peanuts

½ teaspoon (2.5 ml spoon) bicarbonate of soda

1 oz (25 g) butter

Golden peanut-encrusted brittle is fun and very easy to make. This beautiful caramel-coloured candy is a special delight for children. I find it very nice to have on hand, particularly at holiday time.

Grease a baking sheet or a kitchen worktop (the ideal surface is a marble slab). Mix the sugar, syrup and water in a heavy saucepan and cook over a low heat, stirring until the sugar is completely dissolved. Raise the heat slightly and boil the syrup, uncovered, until it reaches a temperature of 295°F/145°C on a sugar thermometer or until a little of the syrup turns very brittle in cold water.

Remove the pan from the heat and stir in the peanuts, soda and butter. Pour the mixture immediately on to the prepared surface and smooth out with a spatula. As the candy cools, stretch it as thin as possible. When cold, break it into irregular pieces for serving.

Sandwiches are very much part of the American way of life and I think most Americans, like myself, have eaten hundreds sitting on the rotating stools of drug store counters. Here are some suggested fillings for (closed) sandwiches as well as a few popular drinks.

Sandwiches

BLT on Wholewheat Toast: 3 crisp rashers of hot bacon (Sainsbury's Tendersweet Streaky Bacon – extra thin rashers – is perfect), slices of tomato, lettuce leaf and 1 tablespoon (15 ml spoon) mayonnaise, between two buttered slices of toasted wholemeal bread.

Peanut Butter and Honey: equal amounts of crunchy peanut butter and honey mixed together.

Tuna Fish Salad: tuna fish mixed with mayonnaise and some finely chopped celery, a little grated apple and a lettuce leaf.

Peanut Butter and Bacon: 3 crisp rashers of hot bacon and a spreading of peanut butter.

Cream Cheese and Jelly: spread with cream cheese and then redcurrant or grape jelly.

Toasted Ham and Cheese: butter both sides of bread and fill with a slice each of ham and Emmenthal cheese. Sauté the sandwich in the frying pan until the outside is toasted and the cheese inside melted.

Drinks

Chocolate Float: whizz together in a blender half a glass of milk, 1 heaped tablespoon (2 × 15 ml spoon) each of Sainsbury's Malted Drink and drinking chocolate and 2 heaped tablespoons (3–4 × 15 ml spoon) chocolate or vanilla ice cream. Serve in a tall glass with a scoop of ice cream floating in it.

Peanut Brittle;
Chocolate Float;
Banana Milkshake;
BLT on Wholewheat
Toast ►

Banana Milkshake: whizz together in a blender 1 small ripe banana, 1 egg and half a glass of milk.

Lemonade: for each ½ pint (300 ml) water add 3 tablespoons (3 × 15 ml spoon) fresh lemon juice and 3–4 tablespoons (3–4 × 15 ml spoon) sugar. Stir and serve with ice.

INDEX TO RECIPES

Design and layout: Ken Vail Graphic Design
Photography: John Lee
Food preparation for photography: Jane Suthering,
Ann Page-Wood
Illustrations: Len Huxter
Typesetting: Westholme Graphics Ltd
Printed and bound by Balding & Mansell Ltd.,
Wisbech, Cambs